LEADING TO WIN

THE MODEL FOR GREAT LEADERSHIP AS DEMONSTRATED BY MILITARY HISTORY AND THE MESSIAH

COLONEL CHRIS PIKE, USAF (RETIRED)

Leading to Win
The Model for Great Leadership
as Demonstrated by Military History and the Messiah

Copyright © 2023 Chris Pike

All rights reserved. Excepting the "Make the Right Choice Worksheet" (Exhibit A in Appendix 2), no part of this publication may be reproduced, distributed, or transmitted in any form or by any means, including photocopying, recording, or other electronic or mechanical methods, without the written permission of the publisher, except in the case of brief quotations properly attributed to this publication for use in critical reviews or scholarly or creative works as permitted by copyright law. For permission requests, write to Yankee Clipper Books "Attention: Permissions Coordinator" at the e-mail address below.

ISBN: 979-8-9881697-0-3 (Paperback)
ISBN: 979-8-9881697-1-0 (Hardcover)
ISBN: 979-8-9881697-2-7 (e-Book)

Library of Congress Control Number: 2023912014

Cover Design by Cherie Foxley at www.cheriefox.com

Printed in the United States of America (The Woodlands, TX)

Yankee Clipper Books LLC
Yankee.clipper.books@gmail.com

DEDICATION

This is dedicated to the two best mentors I ever worked for:

Colonel Virgil Monti, who inspired this book
&
Colonel Bruce Hurd, who coached me through its publication

and to my wife *Libby*, for 25 years of love and support, and for the patience, encouragement and insights that made this book possible.

CONTENTS

*Leadership consists of picking good men
and helping them do their best . . .*

—Fleet Admiral Chester W. Nimitz

1 INTRODUCING LEADING TO WIN

I donned my helmet and flak vest and prepared for combat. This was neither the first nor the last time I wore battle gear, but on this occasion I was wearing it only to bring some humor to what I expected to be a contentious meeting. I was about to walk into the office of Colonel Virgil Monti and offer proposals for how he should reorganize his unit, and I wanted him to know I was ready for any spears that might be thrown my way during the presentation. When he saw me he understood the allusion immediately and laughed heartily. When he was finished, I stopped grinning, put the props aside, and got down to business. I had no idea that day I'd be walking out of the meeting with an inspiration that would help me become a more effective leader and provide the core idea for this book.

* * *

My purpose in writing this book is to share a framework for great leadership that I discovered, developed, and often used to good effect over the long course of my professional careers. I will combine all of my ideas and observations on the subject into a comprehensive model I call **Leading to Win**. There is certainly no shortage of leadership models out there already, and I make no claim to having the "final word" on the subject. But I do hope that readers of this book will reflect on successful leadership a little differently and will consider adopting some of the tools and techniques I describe. I present this model as a series of principles that build upon one another. And because I believe nothing delivers a message better than a good story, I've included engaging stories throughout the book to illustrate each principle. I'll start with this approach right off the bat. As a means of introducing myself and more importantly, of conveying the perspective from which I write, I'll begin with my own "back-story."

I was born in 1966 and grew up in a typical New England middle-class family. I was fortunate enough to be educated in the Connecticut public school system during a time when it had a reputation as one of the best in the country. Within that system I was drawn to history from a very young age. It quickly became my favorite subject, and I was particularly fascinated with military history. I stayed busy outside of school, too, and I had the opportunity to assume various leadership roles throughout my youth—at school, in our church, in my Boy Scout troop, etc. I found I liked leading and moreover, I seemed to be pretty good at it, so I decided I might want to do it for a living.

One of the best places for a leadership-centered career is our military, so when I learned about the American military academy system at age 12, I recognized the unique opportunity these institutions could provide for someone like me. I had no prior connections with the military, but from what I did know about it, I believed it would provide the kind of environment where I'd fit in and likely do well. I therefore set a goal to earn an appointment to the Air Force Academy in Colorado Springs, and I worked steadily toward that goal over the next several years. I did all the things a high school student needs to do to be competitive for a congressional nomination to a service academy: I built a strong academic resume, lettered on the high school track team, and kept busy with extracurricular and community activities that showcased my burgeoning leadership skills. These efforts paid off, for just 16 days after graduating from high school, I found myself in the uniform of an Air Force cadet—at the tender age of 18.

The military academies are regularly referred to as "leadership laboratories" because every cadet or midshipman is pushed to study and demonstrate leadership continuously during four rigorous years of challenging academic coursework and demanding officer training. Each year a few members of the senior class are selected to assume positions as cadet commanders of large units and I was fortunate enough to be appointed to command the 2nd Cadet Squadron. In addition to feeling highly honored to be assigned to this position, I gained enormous practical experience that I would use during my career, including one hard lesson I'll share later. Meanwhile, I continued to pursue my other passion, choosing Military History as a major.

On June 1, 1988, I was commissioned as a second lieutenant in the Air Force. Due to a deterioration of my visual acuity during my cadet years, I was disqualified from pilot training. While this was a big disappointment at the time, it did drive me to look at the broader Air Force for other opportunities to serve in critical leadership positions. After extended research and some soul-searching, I opted to become a transportation officer, in part because this career field choice gave me the opportunity to start leading teams of young, enlisted Airmen immediately.

As the years went by and I grew in rank and experience, I led ever larger teams—with both enlisted and officers assigned—executing ever more complex missions.* In my first six years I progressed through the two lieutenant ranks and then to captain while serving as a front-line leader, interacting directly with the enlisted Airmen performing the core work supporting our squadrons' missions. To provide a reference aid for readers without extensive exposure to the military, I've included Appendix 1 at the end

Here I am as a newly commissioned 2nd lieutenant on Graduation Day, June 1, 1988

---

* For a complete summary of my career history including a list of all my assignments, please see Appendix 3

of the book. It contains tables describing the military rank structure and also explains the hierarchy of military units. I had the opportunity to command units at two of these levels.

An Air Force *squadron* is an organizational unit with all the means to execute a specific functional mission. For example, a fighter squadron would have all the aircraft, pilots, and supporting personnel necessary to launch and fly combat sorties. Likewise, the squadrons within my career field specialty had all the equipment, vehicles, facilities, and trained Airmen required to provide air and ground transportation support on an Air Force base. A squadron is typically the first level in the Air Force organizational hierarchy with an official commander assigned. Following my promotion to the field grade ranks beyond captain, I had the privilege to command the 375th Transportation Squadron at Scott Air Force Base in Illinois as a major, and the 437th Aerial Port Squadron at Charleston Air Force Base in South Carolina as a lieutenant colonel.

The next level above a squadron is a *group*, which is an organization commanded by a colonel and comprised of multiple squadrons with similar or complementary missions. One of the high points of my career was leading over 1,000 Airmen assigned to six squadrons under my command within the 455th Expeditionary Mission Support Group at Bagram Airfield, Afghanistan. At the time I was there – a full year from 2009 to 2010 – this airfield was the most important Allied base in the Afghan War. My group was responsible for keeping the airfield operational and for providing critical support services to the Airmen living there, including security, civil engineering, communications, logistics, and personnel services.

In between these field assignments, I served in a variety of staff roles. I also deployed for several months to the Gulf War in 1991 and to Baghdad, Iraq, in 2006. At key points in my career I returned to the formal classroom setting for professional military education. I rededicated myself to the study of leadership and history as a student, first at the Air Force's Air Command and Staff College and later at the multi-service National War College, which is the Department of Defense's premier war college. After 24 years of active duty and 13 different assignments, I retired from the Air Force in 2012 at the rank of colonel, and embarked upon a second career as a commercial logistics manager in the private sector.

My experience as a military officer and my lifelong study of military history provide me with a wealth of good leadership stories to tell, and I will use some of these stories throughout this book to demonstrate the right or wrong way to employ the leadership model I'll be describing. I sincerely hope this format will also pique my readers' interest in learning more history. I have never lost my fascination with history because the real characters and events I've learned about are more engrossing than the best works of fiction. However, my primary purpose for drawing stories from both history and my personal experiences is to enliven the various concepts I'll present and to make each lesson more compelling. These illuminating stories are also intended to encourage critical thinking from my readers about the Leading to Win principles.

Having referenced the Leading to Win construct several times, it is now time to address the questions many readers are probably asking. What exactly is this construct? How does Leading to Win help leaders succeed? What makes its precepts so special?

Simply put, Leading to Win is an analytical model based on the following series of principles:

- ❖ Principle #1 Frame it up
- ❖ Principle #2 Know your people
- ❖ Principle #3 Hire for quality
- ❖ Principle #4 Put your people in a position to succeed
- ❖ Principle #5 Don't put your people in a position to fail

The coming chapters will define and describe each of these principles in detail and demonstrate how they can work together to help leaders succeed on important tasks. Those chapters will also reveal there is nothing particularly cosmic about Leading to Win. The methodology is quite straight-forward, but it took me several years to recognize all the elements and to internalize their proper application. The journey all started with one core notion, however, which came to me from an off-hand remark. And that brings me back to my meeting with Colonel Monti . . .

The reorganization briefing took place in late 1996, at which time I was a captain serving at Randolph Air Force Base in San Antonio, Texas. This assignment was my fourth duty location in eight years of

The AETC Emblem
(U.S. Air Force)

service. This assignment was different, however, because it was my first experience serving on a headquarters staff. Specifically. I worked at the headquarters of the Air Education and Training Command (AETC). This huge organization, led by a four-star general, was responsible for all education and training activities across the Air Force, including basic training, advanced skills training for every specialty, developmental education, and everything in between.

A brigadier general led the Logistics Directorate and Colonel Monti ran the Logistics Plans Division within it. This is where I worked, two levels below Colonel Monti. Colonel Monti turned out to be one of the best mentors I ever had. He had sound advice for every situation, but was never impressed with himself. He didn't suffer fools easily, but would work with anyone with the right attitude. He kept us focused on our mission while also looking out for each of our needs and goals. And when he believed in someone, he would go to the mat for them. He continued to be an inspiration to me well beyond the two years I worked for him, and when it was time for me to command my first squadron, I strove to emulate a lot of his leadership traits. I'll be sharing more about my relationship with this outstanding professional throughout the book.

My primary duty on the AETC staff was to coordinate planning for all the logistics support required to "bed down" a new aircraft type at a base. This was very rewarding because my work directly enabled the Air Force's newest aircraft to become fully operational at our bases. This job also kept me busy because there were several new weapon systems becoming operational in the late 1990s, including the C-17 transport, the F-22 fighter and the T-6 trainer. Meanwhile, my colleagues in the Logistics Plans Division were working a series of other post-Cold War programs that affected AETC bases and operations. Colonel Monti looked at all the change going on across the Air Force and determined that his division's organizational structure was outdated.

He decided to rearrange the responsibilities among his three branches to streamline our workflow and re-prioritize our programs and duties. He assigned me and the senior noncommissioned officer (NCO)—Chief Master Sergeant Ken Khoma—to work with his whole team and bring him a proposal to address all the specific gaps and problems he had identified. I was told to do this without changing our authorized manpower or expanding our current office space, and I was given a specific timeline to come back and present our findings.

Chief Khoma and I did a deep dive, spoke to everyone on the team, and built a list of proposed changes involving the team structure and the physical realignment of the division's office space. We recognized that some of the folks on the team liked things just as they were, so they might resist our recommendations. I also knew Colonel Monti would be asking probing questions and challenging my assumptions to make sure we had looked at the secondary impacts of each change. All of this potential friction was the impetus for my helmet and flak vest gag.

As I walked Colonel Monti through the plan, I made certain to explain the *why* behind each change and also showed how each proposal met one of his objectives. As expected, he did have some questions, but we had anticipated most of them and had reasonable answers ready. When I was done, we were pleased to find there was not much contention at all, and he approved every significant change we offered. Unexpectedly, then, the planning phase of the project was deemed complete on the spot.

We had been worried we might be sent back to the drawing board, or at the very least, we expected to be asked to rework some major issues and come back for a follow-up. Instead, we had the green light to start implementing the physical and administrative changes immediately. About two weeks later we went live with the new Logistics Plans Division, and the revamped structure proved to be far more effective than what had been in place previously. All these years later, I honestly cannot remember very many of the specific changes we implemented on the project, but I will never forget the observation Colonel Monti made at the very end of the briefing session as Chief Khoma and I were getting ready to leave his office:

"I have said it over and over: If you want a task done right, then assign the right person to do it!"

That comment was obviously meant as an accolade for the work we had done and I recognized it as such at that moment, but over time I came to realize he had given me much more than a spot compliment. His words made a profound impression upon me that day, and as my career progressed, I came to see how absolutely true they were. Looking back years later, I can see how I had applied—or failed to apply—this advice as a young leader. Moreover, as I assumed ever-more-senior leadership positions, I began to very deliberately employ this principle to accomplish the unit's mission and deliver on important projects. By the time I retired, I would often repeat Colonel Monti's words whenever someone asked me, "What is the secret to effective leadership?"

As pithy as this answer may be, executing it properly can be more complicated than it sounds. Anyone can assign people to tasks, but only a truly astute leader will consistently assign the right people to the right tasks. Such leaders often appear to have an instinctive ability to achieve a successful outcome on any project or challenge, but in reality these leaders have mastered a mindset that propels favorable outcomes. Delivering the right results with a high degree of regularity is exactly what Leading to Win is all about, but until a leader comprehends and embraces the principles described in this book, the likelihood of getting desired results is about equal to what random chance would yield. The succeeding chapters of this book will help leaders understand, develop, and eventually perfect their own Leading to Win mindset.

2. WHAT IS GREAT LEADERSHIP?

Winston Churchill, Franklin Roosevelt, Martin Luther King Jr., Mahatma Gandhi, Albert Einstein, Margaret Thatcher, Nelson Mandela, Mother Teresa, Wangari Maathai and Ronald Reagan. According to Jan-Benedict Steenkamp, a renowned speaker and author of the book *Time to Lead: Lessons for Today's Leaders from Bold Decisions that Changed History*, these are the top 10 leaders of the 20th century.[1]

Mr. Steenkamp's list infers that great leaders come from a variety of backgrounds, cultures and vocations. While I suspect most people would agree with that, I also suspect that like me, many readers questioned why various people were or were not included on the list. As a military history buff, for instance, I am disappointed that Mr. Steenkamp chose not to include a single military leader in the group. Others may have similar objections. In fact, I doubt any two people asked to name their own Top 10 would create the same list because evaluating leadership is a highly subjective endeavor.

Leadership requires a mix of intellectual, administrative, technical, political, and people skills, all interacting with each other at the same time, and all nearly impossible to measure objectively. Only a few people over the ages have been able to master enough of these traits to be counted among the truly "great" leaders of history, but again, there is little consensus as to who these few people are. It seems that every admirer of a great leader has a corresponding detractor who doesn't consider that leader "great" at all. In the absence of a set of agreed-upon metrics, then, the perception of who exhibits great leadership is all too often in the eye of the beholder. An attempt to identify and define every aspect of leadership, and then assign an objective standard for "greatness" to each would produce a work running to several volumes, and there would still be plenty of room for debate among the readers. This book is much less ambitious. It will instead utilize an intentionally *narrow* definition of successful leadership, one which came together for me only after several years of reflection.

* * *

This process of defining great leadership began with what was essentially a daydream. When I was devouring military biographies as a young officer, I asked myself, "If I someday end up in the history books as an accomplished military leader, who would I want to be compared to?"

It goes without saying that I wanted to be counted among the great ones, if possible, so after I read each biography I'd assess the subject's greatness. I really had no methodology or even logical basis for how I classified each person. I simply reacted to what I had learned and selected the ones that impressed me the most. I ultimately gave General of the Army George C. Marshall the #1 ranking on my personal roster of history's greatest military leaders. Among the list of prominent duty titles he held throughout his life were Army Chief of Staff, Chairman of the Joint Chiefs of Staff in World War II, Secretary of State, and Secretary of Defense. We'll revisit General Marshall and explore his accomplishments in a coming chapter, where we'll also watch him demonstrate his mastery of the Leading to Win principles.

So what was it about Marshall and the other leaders I admired that made them appear "great" in my eyes? Back in my starry-eyed youth, I didn't have a broad enough perspective to answer this precisely, but fortunately I was not yet leading at a high enough level where it mattered. What *did* matter was that I was already thinking about such things. Young leaders can benefit greatly when they have an insatiable curiosity about how to become ever-better leaders, so the time I dedicated to studying the traits of possible role models from history was very well-spent.

Another valuable source of wisdom on the topic of leadership is direct contact with established leaders serving in the present time, so my peers and I were always on the lookout for opportunities to glean advice from such people. As it turned out, I got just the intellectual infusion I needed when one of those opportunities arose. The impact of this experience was substantial, for it allowed me to craft a personal definition of successful leadership that has remained with me ever since.

It began one afternoon when I joined a group of my colleagues at a guest-speaking engagement featuring a well-respected general officer. The general's take-away point sounded very profound when we heard it:

"The highest priority task of every leader is to prepare the next generation of leaders."

Here was something to take home and ponder, so I did. I thought about both the statement and the implied activities a leader must do to build the next generation of leaders. Some key activities I determined should be on the list were these:

- Build time into the schedule for formal mentoring and leadership training
- Determine the skills each person lacks and provide experiences that will help them develop those skills
- Personally counsel them about the best assignments for advancement along their career path
- Assess everyone's long-term prospects and make sure the leaders with the highest potential stand out

I would eventually do all these things as I guided the development of younger officers later in my career, so the general's message gave me great food for thought on the importance of building for the future. In a very real way, his speech to us that day put his own words into action because it helped to develop my generation for future leadership roles by forcing us to think about how we could help progress the leadership capabilities of the young officers we would be serving with later.

However, after deeper reflection I felt conflicted about the general's main assertion, and I finally concluded it was wrong. Although identifying and advising young leaders is very important strategically and well worth doing, I determined *the true first priority of any leader must be accomplishing today's mission*. An NFL coach who makes every season a "building year" probably won't keep his job, nor will his team ever win a Super Bowl. Similarly, a business manager who invests heavily in personal mentoring but never hits the quarterly plan won't be first in line for annual bonuses. Taking this to an extreme, I imagined a battalion commander in the midst of a pitched battle telling his executive officer to bring in all the company commanders for a meeting:

> "Yes, Sir," says the executive officer, "I assume you want to confirm their orders so we can take the hill and complete our assigned mission?"
>
> "No, we'll worry about that later. For now, I want to go over how to do an effective counseling session for a sub-standard performer. I think they need more work in that area, so they'll be better battalion commanders in seven or eight years. Don't ever forget the first priority of every leader!"

Although this scenario is intentionally ridiculous, it does demonstrate how far off course we might drift when we emphasize the wrong priorities of leadership. I ultimately concluded leaders are given their roles so they can produce results in the here-and-now, and that is why this book defines great leadership specifically in terms of *effective mission accomplishment*. I still stand by this characterization, but with the wisdom of hindsight, I now recognize that accomplishing today's mission and developing young leaders are two interdependent imperatives that should happen simultaneously, especially within the Leading to Win framework. I'll expound on this dynamic in greater detail in Chapter 4.

Once I came to grips with the question of leadership's primary purpose, I was able to identify what all the great leaders on my own list had in common. When I read their biographies, I could not help but be impressed by the sheer number of feats they accomplished and the magnitude of their significance. I was lionizing individuals who took on challenge after challenge, often under daunting conditions, and repeatedly led huge organizations to success. To me, it was the seemingly relentless ability to accomplish big missions that made these leaders stand out, and that characteristic became the basis of my Leading to Win construct.

For the purposes of this book, I define "successful leadership" as ***the ability to consistently lead teams to do important tasks right*** and "great leaders" are those who do this particularly well. These great leaders are easy to spot. They are the leaders who always bring out the most from every member of their teams. They are the leaders whose teams can seemingly solve any problem. They are the leaders with the reputation for constantly delivering what the organization needs. The goal of this book is to help build such leaders.

A **task** can be almost anything: attaining a combat objective in wartime, launching a new product or business line, increasing learning proficiency at an educational institution, renovating a historic building, or providing critical services to an underprivileged community, to name just a few. Moreover, the task need not be as grandiose as these examples—it just has to be important. Of course, what makes a task important is also often subjective, so this book will define an "important task" as one that *must have a successful outcome*, irrespective of its scope or complexity. In other words, the results have to *matter* to the organization.

The *right* results are defined by the person who envisioned the task in the first place, so a successful outcome is one that meets the desired end state. Organizations often use terms such as "delivering" or "producing" or "achieving" to declare victory for a task, but in this book we will call it **winning.** Leaders who want to win—frequently and repeatedly – can do so by applying the Leading to Win practices I'll outline in the following chapters.

I have already mentioned that I will be sharing personal anecdotes from my Air Force career as well as military history vignettes throughout the book to help elucidate these principles, but be assured I do not mean to imply that Leading to Win practices are limited to just military leaders or military organizations. On the contrary, they are *universal* in their application. This model will work for leaders at any level of any organization. Imagine any setting where someone is responsible for managing a team: a factory, a church, a merchant vessel at sea, a college, a sports team, a charity event, a corporate office, the local DMV, etc. These are all places where the leader can apply this model and win. Furthermore, Leading to Win also applies universally to any task, for great leadership does not depend on a task's nature or purpose. What great leadership *does* dependent on—and what the remainder of this book will concentrate on—is the analytical approach a great leader uses to accomplish the task.

Before we begin this journey, however, I need to address an important point. Some readers may be troubled with my singular emphasis on task *outcomes*. Many of us know people who regularly get the job done, but only by leaving a swath of human wreckage in their wake. If my model would allow us to classify those people as great leaders, some readers may be tempted to put the book down now and dismiss Leading to Win before we even get started. To preclude that, I will address this concern right now.

First of all, I firmly believe that great leaders treat others with dignity, especially the people they lead. Therefore, abusing people is absolutely *not* the way to get a job done "right." Secondly, although this book is about exploring the means to achieve desired outcomes, I want to reemphasize that great leaders must be masters of many skills. While we are not going to delve into all these other attributes in this book, let's agree that all truly great leaders possess reliable moral compasses, treat their people with genuine respect and concern, and care as much about the organization's prospects as their own advancement. If we further agree that any leader who wants to adopt this book's ideas also shares these attributes, then we should be free to set about exploring the Leading to Win concepts on their own merits and without reservations.

CASE STUDY: THE MESSIAH

To reinforce this notion that the Leading to Win methodology can be used by any leader in any organization at any time with the same prospects for success, I will close each succeeding chapter with an on-going case study of a single character who had no association with the military lifestyle at all. The case study will evaluate the use of Leading to Win principles by a great religious and spiritual leader executing a critical mission—Jesus of Nazareth.

The idea of using Jesus as the subject and calling the case study "The Messiah" occurred to me when I recognized that Jesus' own (very successful) leadership style often employed the same principles I am writing about. Full disclosure: I am a committed Christian who believes Jesus is the resurrected Son of God. That said, this case study will still work for all readers no matter their religious beliefs because I will be analyzing Jesus' actions as a *human leader* rather than offering any sort of theological discourse.

I think almost everyone can agree the historical Jesus is a worthy subject for this book simply because he changed the world on a scale matched by few others. The far-reaching movement he inspired remains relevant 20 centuries after his own time, and it is the successful launching of that movement that will serve as the great mission we will explore in the case study. I will demonstrate how the Leading to Win concepts presented in each chapter were integral to Jesus' strategy.

For the case to work, however, I do ask that you indulge me in one respect. Because the Bible's gospels and the book of *Acts* are the definitive sources describing the detailed life and actions of Jesus and his followers, I will treat them as historically accurate documents. I cannot highlight Jesus' creative use of Leading to Win without referencing the Biblical chronicle, nor will the case study remain coherent if I exclude the "supernatural" elements from the stories.

Readers who believe the Bible is literally true can simply take it at face value, while I would ask those readers who do not share this opinion of the Bible to instead view the incidents described as allegorical. A start from either of these perspectives or from anywhere in between will bring us all to the same end point, which is a series of rich leadership lessons. Irrespective of each reader's personal beliefs as to whether or not Jesus was the "messiah," I think we'll see that he has much to teach us all about great leadership.

Finally, one last disclaimer: after reading this book, you may be able to emulate some of Jesus' leadership style, but you will *not* be able to change wine into water, raise the dead or give sight to the blind . . .

3 THE TASK

Principle #1: Frame It Up

One day very early in my career, I was having lunch with a fellow lieutenant. She was clearly a little frustrated, so I asked what was bothering her. She said, "Well, it's my boss Major Nebulus. He's not a bad guy, but he's very hard to work for. He'll call me in and describe something he wants me to do for him, but he's very vague. He tells me, 'I'm not sure exactly what I want, but I'll know it when I see it.' I'm now on my third attempt trying to give him what he's looking for, and I still don't really know what I'm supposed to do!"

I fortunately never had to work directly for a Major Nebulus, but during my career I did see that style of task management used by more than a few leaders. At one point I worked on a staff where the previous director had told his people, "I shouldn't have to tell you what I want all the time. You should be able to read my vibe." Needless to say, staff efficiency during his tenure was not very high.

Not coincidentally, few leaders who used this approach established stellar reputations for winning, nor did their people thrive in their roles. Instead, many of them felt like they were spinning their wheels, as they wasted a lot of time and effort that too often achieved nothing. If a leader really wants a job done right, that leader must ensure everyone knows what the job is and what "right" should look like. It all starts with the task.

In the last chapter I indicated that Leading to Win does not depend upon the nature or scope of a task. And while that is true, it is also true that the people assigned to do a specific task are *highly* dependent upon the features of the task. If they hope to accomplish the mission successfully, they must know what the mission is and what the proper result will be. It is incumbent upon leaders to establish a process for providing their people with the guidance they need to win. Leaders must become experts at **framing** their tasks.

*   *   *

Framing the task simply means defining the task in a manner so the person working the task doesn't have to wonder what the leader really wants. It is important that a leader always follows the principle of properly framing a task, but there is no one right way to execute it. That said, I do recommend using a formal framing document if the task is at all complex. I personally developed a framing process that was inspired by the "one minute goal" introduced in *The One Minute Manager* by Ken Blanchard and Spencer Johnson.[2] In that book, the fictional manager's technique was to issue his staff a set of verbal instructions used to describe a task – in one minute or less. To ensure more precise communications, I adapted the concept by issuing a short set of *written* instructions that described all the important aspects of the task.

While I was serving as the commander of the aerial port squadron at Charleston, I used this framing template repeatedly to assign tasks aimed at enhancing the operational excellence of our unit. As a rule, I tried to limit my framings to no more than two pages, although some ran to a third page when additional detail was required. If the document stretched beyond that, it prompted me to start editing to preserve brevity and clarity. Because every task was unique, the final structure of each framing varied somewhat, too, but they were always built around four critical elements. I encourage all leaders to adopt whatever framing tool best fits their needs and personalities, but I also strongly recommend they incorporate these same elements into their framing in some form or fashion.

ELEMENT 1: OBJECTIVE

The essential starting point for every leader is to define the **objective**. A Leading to Win objective is a statement of intent for the task—it describes *what* must be done and what success should look like when the task is complete. In this book the objective represents the mission to accomplish, or the goal to be achieved, but other leaders may choose to call it something else. The terminology used isn't critical, but the effective communication of the objective statement within the framing is. To borrow from the Latin, a good objective description is the *sine qua non*—"without which, then nothing"—for the entire task.

Although not required in every case, a leader may want to include within the objective statement some comments about the broader purpose of the task. A simple explanation about *why* the task matters can help the team understand the full context, enabling them to deliver an outcome tailored to the circumstances. For example, when I was commanding my group in Afghanistan I had an embedded civil engineer squadron for the primary purpose of keeping the airfield in good repair. One day I directed the unit to construct a vehicle parking area for an Army organization on base, a task that would normally have been considered out of scope for this unit's mission. Without more context the tasking may have caused some confusion about prioritization of resources available to do the project. Therefore, along with the specific requirements for the parking area, I also included language explaining that the project was part of a larger agreement with the Army to free up some prime real estate for the Air Force's needs elsewhere on the airfield. Telling my team "the rest of the story" allowed them to plan, schedule, and execute the mission more efficiently.

Sometimes the objective statement can be short and the required outcome self-evident. "Take the hill," for instance, is the quintessential military phrase for this case. However, even enormous tasks can have concise mission statements. When General Dwight Eisenhower was first appointed as Supreme Allied Commander of the D-Day invasion in World War II, he received this objective statement within a one-page mission directive: "You will enter the continent of Europe and in conjunction with other Allied nations, undertake operations aimed at the heart of Germany and the destruction of her armed forces."[3] Those few words defined Eisenhower's goal and the desired results. He was to invade mainland Europe and vanquish the enemy. In this case neither Ike (nor anyone else on the Allied side of the war) needed any additional context about *why* this task was important, so none was included.*

General Eisenhower meets with his paratroopers in June 1944, just before their D-Day jumps (Library of Congress)

In cases where tasks cannot be fully expressed in a single sentence, the leader should provide an extended explanation that may comprise many lines or even several paragraphs. The objective statements General Eisenhower sent to his subordinates for their particular D-Day missions followed this model. They were much more detailed and specific and often included **sub-tasks** within the over-arching mission. While sub-tasks are not required in every case, they can be very helpful, especially when they are prerequisites to mission accomplishment. In my parking lot directive to the civil engineers, for example, I included a sub-task to construct a perimeter fence with a lockable gate. Had I not specified that, the engineers could have presented me with a "finished" lot that was unsecured, and therefore did not meet the Army's full requirement.

Judicious use of sub-tasks can also serve to outline the path to mission success on a more complex task. However, excessive use of sub-tasks or very long objective statements may actually be a sign that the leader is using the objective statement to tell the team *how* to do

---

* When the Germans finally surrendered to him, Eisenhower sent an equally concise reply to his leadership: "The mission of the Allied Force was fulfilled at 0241 local time, May 7th, 1945"

the task, and that is a mistake. During Basic Cadet Training at the Air Force Academy, we had to memorize a series of leadership quotes. One of my favorites came from General George Patton, who advised "Never tell people *how* to do things. Tell them *what* to do and let them surprise you with their ingenuity."[4] I recommend Patton's advice be the guiding principle here, too—tell the team what to do in the objective statement and if the leader believes there must be guidance on how to do it, those inputs are better included in a different part of the framing.

Irrespective of the length or the specific structure employed for the objective statement, the most important thing is that the mission must be clear and the end state precise. One of history's most infamously muddled orders came from General Robert E. Lee at a critical point during the Battle of Gettysburg. Ironically, it was literally a "take the hill" order—or at least we think it was . . .

Everything that led up to the crucial moment in this story started several weeks before at the Battle of Chancellorsville, among the most brilliant victories of Lee's career. Thanks to the audacious leadership of Lee's 2nd Corps commander Lieutenant General Thomas "Stonewall" Jackson, the confederates pulled off a stunning victory that completely shocked the Union's Army of the Potomac. However, the victory cost Lee dearly, for Jackson was wounded by friendly fire and died a few days later. The loss of Jackson, perhaps the best battlefield commander on either side of the Civil War, would plague Lee for the rest of the war.

Following the battle and the loss of Jackson, Lee did two things. He first re-organized the Army of Northern Virginia into a three-corps army, promoting Richard Ewell and A.P. Hill to lieutenant generals and placing them in charge of the 2nd and 3rd Corps, respectively. He then convinced Confederate President Jefferson Davis to authorize a new invasion of the North. Lee planned to follow up his victory with a strike into Pennsylvania, where he could forage for supplies, bring the war "home" to Northern civilians, threaten Harrisburg and Philadelphia, and maneuver into a strong position from which to fight another battle with the Army of the Potomac. Lee did not believe the demoralized Army of the Potomac would recover quickly, so he expected to have free rein in enemy territory for quite a while before he'd have to fight again.

By the end of June 1863, Lee had pushed his army into central Pennsylvania, where he was indeed moving about freely with no sign of the Union army. On July 1st, the leading elements of both armies stumbled across each other at a country crossroads and began a fight that neither commanding general was expecting. This surprise encounter above the town of Gettysburg would soon grow into the largest battle ever fought in North America.

As the clamor of battle grew louder, troops from both armies marched toward the sound of the guns and threw themselves into the fight. Lee's troops won the race and eventually overwhelmed the Union forces at that location. When the line broke, the survivors ran pell-mell through the town with the southerners in hot pursuit. Fortunately for the fleeing soldiers, two other Union corps had arrived and taken a strong position south of town on the high ground known as Cemetery Ridge. The fleeing soldiers who made it through the town saw their fellow blue coats atop Cemetery Ridge and joined them there, falling into defensive positions Major General Oliver Howard had been preparing throughout the day. Meanwhile, the energized Confederates, now commanded by General Ewell, had followed and were assembling not far from the hill. Ewell looked up at the formidable obstacle before him and pondered what to do next.

Meanwhile, General Lee was still well back from the actual fighting, but he had been receiving regular reports as he hurried toward the scene. Although Lee had been directing his generals to avoid embroiling the army in a major action all day in case the entire Union army was just over the horizon, he recognized he now had a real opportunity. If Ewell could dislodge the Union forces from Cemetery Ridge, the federal army would have nowhere to go except backwards, and this battle could be another lopsided Confederate victory, in a Northern state to boot! Lee sent a courier riding to Ewell with his orders:

"Take the hill, if practicable, but don't bring on a general engagement."

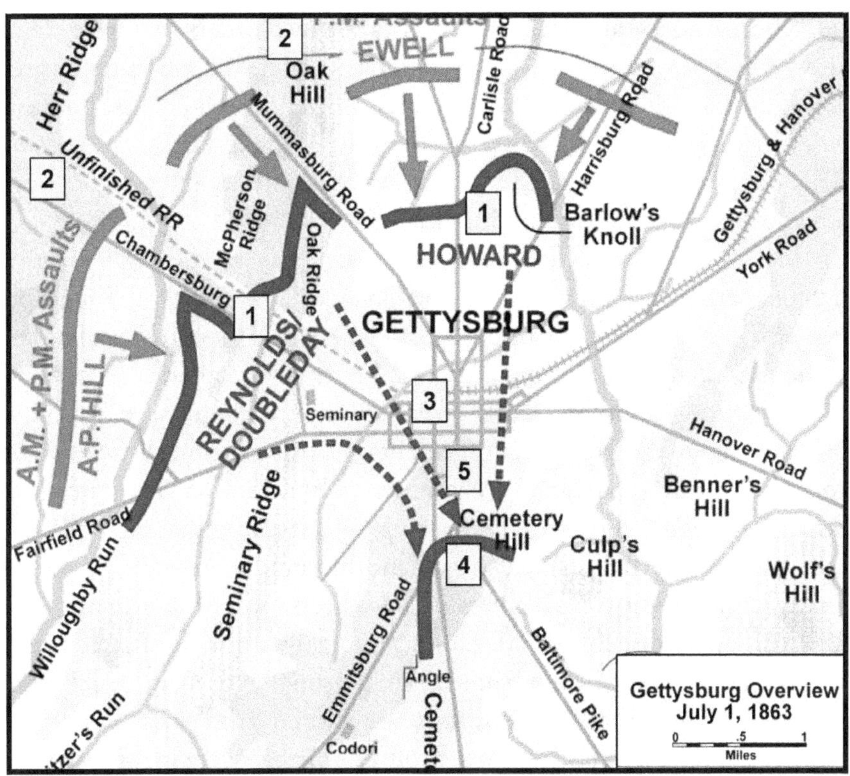

On July 1, 1863, two Union corps took positions north and west of town (1) to block Confederate forces converging on Gettysburg from those directions. After several hours of tough fighting the Confederates amassed enough troops to overwhelm the Union, forcing the collapse of their lines in the late afternoon. (2) The Union soldiers retreated through the city streets of Gettysburg (3), pursued closely by the victorious Confederates. The Union men who escaped their pursuers took refuge on the high ground south of the town, which their fellow bluecoats had been fortifying all day. (4) When Confederate General Ewell emerged from the town around 5 PM, he was faced with the sight of a formidable Union presence occupying a strong defensive position atop Cemetery Ridge. Ewell received Lee's cryptic order shortly thereafter. (5)

(Map by Hal Jespersen, www.cwmaps.com)

General Ewell had a reputation for coarse language and one can only imagine he let loose some colorful words when he received these orders. He had previously served as one of Stonewall Jackson's division commanders, and Jackson had always issued orders that were clear and peremptory, but this was neither. Lee's order was a monument to ambiguity, and it completely confounded Ewell. He likely had no idea whether Lee wanted him to act aggressively and take a risk for a potentially big reward or intended him to be more cautious and avoid taking large losses or escalating the situation.

In hindsight, most historians agree that Lee wanted Ewell to storm the hill, perhaps adding "if practicable" as an out for Ewell if the attempt was proving too costly and he needed to pull back. However, Ewell never made the attempt at all, likely because he thought the federal position was too strong and any attack on that position would have certainly brought about the general engagement Lee warned him to avoid. Of course, this last qualifier in Lee's order only added to the confusion because everyone who had been fighting at Gettysburg that day believed they had crossed the general engagement threshold hours earlier!

We'll never know if Ewell would have been successful, even though his decision has been second-guessed by analysts for the last century and a half. Some have even blamed him personally for losing the Battle of Gettysburg at that moment, but the real fault lies with Lee. Had Lee been more precise with the text of his objective statement, perhaps ordering Ewell to "Storm the hill immediately and continue the assault until the position is taken or there is no prospect of success," American history as we know it may well have changed dramatically. It is not a stretch to argue that Lee's failure to issue an effective objective statement cost the Confederacy its last chance to win independence. Some 80 years later, however, at another critical moment during another great war, we find a perfect example of how to do this right . . .

General Dwight Eisenhower led the invasions of North Africa and Sicily before he was named Supreme Allied Commander for Operation OVERLORD, the cross-channel invasion of Europe planned for the spring of 1944. Eisenhower decided to bring some of the key officers he had worked with on those earlier campaigns to his new command, including Air Force generals Carl Spaatz and Jimmy Doolittle. He named Spaatz to a new senior air position, and he eventually agreed with Spaatz's recommendation to assign Doolittle as commander of the mighty 8th Air Force in England. However, 8th Air Force already had a commander in Lieutenant General Ira Eaker, who had built that fabled command from the ground up.

Thus, Eaker was being displaced just at the point where he believed his creation could really start to make an impact on the war, an impact that was, however, already overdue. There were a number of valid reasons why 8th Air Force had not yet delivered on its promise, but Eisenhower was more interested in looking forward than backward, and he envisioned using air power differently in the run-up to D-Day. First and foremost, he needed to gain air superiority over France, or his troops would be massacred before they ever reached the shore. Eisenhower did not believe 8th Air Force's single-minded campaign of strategic bombing could deliver this, so he wanted a new approach. Doolittle had earned his place in history by leading the famous "Thirty Seconds Over Tokyo" raid in 1942, and now Eisenhower needed him to do something equally bold to get the full potential out of 8th Air Force.

General Doolittle soon found the opportunity to do that by changing the objective statement for his fighter pilots. As he himself explained it, "The mission of the [fighter] escorts was unequivocal at that time: protect the bombers and not leave them. This policy concerned me because fighter aircraft are designed to go after enemy fighters. Fighter pilots are usually pugnacious individuals by nature and are trained to be aggressive in the air. Their machines are specifically designed for offensive action. I thought our fighter forces should intercept the enemy fighters before they reached the bombers. The 'don't leave the bombers' escort philosophy came to a halt when I visited Major General William E. "Bill" Kepner's 8th Fighter Command. On the wall of his office was a sign: THE FIRST DUTY OF THE EIGHTH AIR FORCE FIGHTERS IS TO BRING THE BOMBERS BACK ALIVE."[5] Doolittle ordered the sign be torn down immediately and replaced with a new one that read, "THE FIRST DUTY OF THE EIGHTH AIR FORCE FIGHTERS IS TO DESTROY GERMAN FIGHTERS." From that moment forward, American fighters would be on the offensive in the air war.

Not surprisingly, the bomber crews did not care for this new objective at first, but in very short order, Doolittle's directive paid out huge dividends for the Allies. The fighter pilots were let off their leashes and

Lieutenant General Jimmy Doolittle with his 8th Air Force fliers (U.S Air Force)

they went after the Luftwaffe with a vengeance, attacking (and destroying) the German fighters well away from the bomber formations. By the end of the "Big Week" air offensive in February 1944, 8th Air Force had achieved sufficient command of the air to allow the bombers to finally strike targets at will and do even more damage. Allied air power softened up the pending battlefields all over Western Europe, and when the troops hit the beaches at Normandy on June 6, 1944, the skies were virtually devoid of German aircraft. Mission accomplished!

Long or short, with or without context or sub-tasks, an explicit objective statement is absolutely essential in Leading to Win.

ELEMENT 2: MILESTONES & TIMELINES

Milestones & timelines comprise the second element of the framing process. These are not always necessary or practical, but they should be included if the leader expects the task completion to proceed in stages. While the objective statement addresses the *what* and *why* of the task, the milestones & timelines section defines the *how* and the *when*, if needed.

As a minimum, the leader will normally provide a final date for task accomplishment, and if that is the only timeline detail needed, then it can be woven into the objective statement itself. However, if the leader intends to have periodic reviews of progress or wants to direct specific and sequential actions the team must take, then he'll want to include a stand-alone milestones & timelines entry. For instance, one of my Charleston framing documents called for creating a syllabus for on-the-job training (OJT) of our young Airmen. The Air Force's program was already clear on the skills and the standards required for fulfilling OJT requirements, but there was no consistency in the management of the training itself. Indeed, I concluded there really was no management of the process at all because our Airmen were essentially left on their own to find a certified trainer and get qualified on each OJT task whenever they could.

This approach was plainly inefficient, but I was also convinced the randomness of the task completion process was undermining the learning process. I used the milestones & timelines section in this framing to clearly direct how the project team should build the new syllabus. I fudged on Patton's rule here a little, but as the whole syllabus concept was completely foreign to the people on the team, I needed to coach them on the project management aspects of the task. They had the technical expertise and the experience to know how best to arrange the tasks in the syllabus, but they needed some step-by-step instructions to understand how to pull it all together. I made each step a milestone and its due date a timeline item.

This OJT Syllabus project proved its worth after the first tranche of Airmen went through the program. We had no Airmen on "probation" because they were behind their training schedule and in fact, almost all of them completed the full program a couple of months early. Moreover, the quality of the training clearly was better, too, for the majority of our trainees earned end-of-course test scores above 90%. Prior to implementing the syllabus, breaking 90% was a rare feat and considered an "honors level" achievement. We made that level of performance commonplace.

As big a win as the OJT enhancements were for my unit, it was still a fairly minor project compared to, say, the greatest amphibious operation in history. The orders sent to Eisenhower referenced earlier in the chapter had just a single timeline, "the month of May 1944,"[6] which was the target date for the invasion. Eisenhower was left to self-define the milestones to fulfill his objective. The final plans he issued to his subordinate commanders for their D-Day objectives, however, were incredibly detailed in terms of both milestones and timelines. Every task is unique, and some won't require time-driven elements at all, but when milestones & timelines are needed, embedding them in the framing will increase the likelihood of accomplishing the mission.

ELEMENT 3: RESOURCES

Giving a team a destination to reach with no means to get there is a sure-fire way to sabotage success. In many cases, the team will need specific **resources**—people, funding, equipment, supplies, access to needed information, etc. Resources available for the task are allocated in the third section of the framing. Note that in my story from Chapter 1 about the reorganization of the Logistics Plans Division, Colonel Monti specifically told us we could not increase our personnel or our office space. Without that guidance we might have come back with an organizational plan calling for more employees or assuming access to additional facilities, neither of which were possible. By defining the resource constraints up front, Colonel Monti ensured we proposed only feasible solutions. A good leader therefore should identify the resources available for the task from the outset or the team will drive down the road to failure because the plan is unsound.

For this section of the framing, the format is simple—list the various resources that will be made available and in what quantities. The strategic military planning enterprise does this very deliberately, using a document called the Time-Phased Force Deployment Data Listing (TPFDDL, pronounced "tip-fiddle"). Every important operational or contingency plan starts with an allocation of the specific forces that can be made available for the operation. These military units are assigned on the presumption that they can only support one plan at a time, and during the 1990s our entire military force structure was based on the requirement to execute two major theater wars (MTWs) simultaneously. That is, we had to man enough units to fight the two MTWs independently, so a single unit such as the 82nd Airborne Division could not be on the TPFDDL of both war plans.

Each plan's TPFDDL defines the personnel and equipment resources a warzone commander will have for the fight. But before they can fight, all those forces have to move to the battlefield, and that takes two other precious resources—time and strategic transport assets. The number of ships and aircraft that will be available to move the forces is also specified in the war plan as a constraint that defines the "time-phased" part of the listing. It can take weeks or even months to transport all the forces in the plan. The combat theater commander must therefore develop a battle plan that will work with only the forces he will have in place at any given moment until the deployment is complete. There is a reason that creating a major operational plan takes many months and a whole lot of people and advanced modeling tools, but it is worth the effort. Without knowing the resources assigned, no commander would be able to meet the objective statement.

The availability of resources often drives the milestones & timelines. For instance, the D-Day invasion actually took place a month later than the target date in Eisenhower's order, primarily for one specific reason. The Allies were able to provide the forces needed for the Channel crossing and the landings at Normandy, but not the means to get everything onto the beaches. There simply were not enough landing craft—specifically landing ship tanks (LSTs)—to bring all the required equipment ashore. The shortage of LSTs became the limiting factor for the entire operation. General Eisenhower was faced with the

LSTs offloading their cargo on the D-Day Beaches. These vessels were critical to the success of the operation and became the limiting factor for when the invasion could launch. (U.S. Naval History and Heritage Command)

choice of attacking sooner, but with a much smaller landing force, or delaying the invasion until the Allies could build and assemble enough landing craft. He and the Allied leadership wisely chose the latter course, and the plan worked.

Most leaders are fortunately not faced with the task of fighting a major war with limited forces and extended timelines to get them in place, but they still need to understand the constraints limiting their task completion so they can plan for them and mitigate their impact on the task. Where there are resource requirements to accomplish a task, those resources must be specified in the framing.

ELEMENT 4: AUTHORITIES

The final element of the framing concerns the **authorities** that come with the tasking. This section is often self-evident, especially if the task is within the normal scope of the responsibilities of the project team members. However, including guidance on authorities can be very useful to the team members for broad tasks with "fuzzy" organizational lines.

For instance, when Colonel Monti assigned me to work his reorganization project, he made it clear that I was acting with his authority during the research stage. I was junior to many of the people from whom I was gathering information and I was not even a member of the other two branches in the division. Without a public announcement of the project to all personnel, I could well have been stone-walled by people who didn't want any change or just didn't think they needed to spend time answering my questions. By the same token, he made it clear to me I had the authority within the project only to *propose* changes, while he would approve and direct the final structure.

Defining clear authorities prevents what I call the Two Sins of Authority Misuse. Most people are familiar with the First Sin, which is when individuals try to assume authority they *do not* have. This rarely ends well, because it creates resentment among those being imposed upon, with a predictable reaction. How often are the expressions, "Who died and made you boss?" or "I don't work for you" followed by "So how can I help you?" Instead, the offender usually gets a cold shoulder rather than the help he needs, making it more difficult for the team to complete key actions for mission accomplishment.

The Second Sin of Authority Misuse is less obvious, but can also be debilitating for the team. This sin is the chronic inability of people to use the authority they *do* have. A person who has the power to make decisions and give directions, but fails to do so, can grind progress to a halt because important activities cannot move forward. In many cases this inaction comes from a person's lack of confidence about whether they actually have the authority at all. Formal designation of the authority will alleviate this problem. Of course, when someone is still too afraid to use the authority they know they have, the leader has a different problem. Such indecisiveness is usually a loud warning sign that the wrong person has been put on the task, so the leader's best course of action is to take back the authority from the person who has it and give it to someone else as quickly as possible.

The military generally does a very good job defining authorities at all levels. For instance, in the war plan scenarios described above, the theater commander has very broad authority over all the final battlefield decisions, but that authority applies only within the geographical boundaries of the command and to the forces assigned there. The Pacific theater commander cannot, for example, order a squadron of aircraft in England to move to Guam. Because bad things can and do happen to leaders in war, proper plans also include command succession, that is, they specify who will assume command should anything happen to the primary commander. To examine a perfect case of what happens when the leader fails to account for authorities in a framing, let's return to the Civil War Battle of Chancellorsville . . .

After a series of intractable, uninspired or downright incompetent commanders of the Union's Army of the Potomac, President Lincoln appointed Major General Joseph Hooker to take command in the spring of 1863. Hooker did a very thorough job of re-organizing the Army, improving intelligence operations and implementing special training for "light" units that could move quickly to critical points on the battlefield. As he played cat and mouse with Lee's army, it became apparent they would clash near the little hamlet of Chancellorsville, Virginia. Hooker assembled a solid battle plan and made sure each corps commander had clarity on his role in the battle. The Army was probably in a better position to win a face-to-face battle against Lee than it had ever been up to that point. Unfortunately for the Union, though, Hooker made two key mistakes. He did not establish a clear succession plan and he chose not to share his grand battle plan with his key generals.

Once the battle kicked off, it was hard-fought by the greatly out-numbered Confederates, but the Union was still in the best position to win as long as all the corps contributed where needed, but that information was too often known only to Hooker. When Stonewall Jackson took his corps on a desperate end-around maneuver and destroyed Hooker's right flank just before sundown, all semblance of Hooker's original battle plan was gone and the whole army started to lose cohesiveness. The Union recovered somewhat overnight, but Hooker continued to play things close to the vest. His army paid for this lack of transparency the next morning when Hooker was wounded by flying debris from enemy cannon fire and knocked unconscious at a critical moment in the battle.

Major General Darius Couch was next in seniority and so should have immediately taken command, but the transition was poorly handled and for a critical hour, the Union army was effectively leaderless. When Hooker woke up, he remained concussed and clearly confused for several more hours, during which time Couch was nominally in command. However, Hooker had been just lucid enough for just long enough to forbid Couch from making any independent decisions. Moreover, even if Couch had assumed full command, he had no better idea of what Hooker planned to do at that point than anyone else on the battlefield. Meanwhile, Hooker had not shared enough of the plan with the various other corps commanders, either, so even if they had been given any latitude to act on their own initiative, they probably would not have known how best to help the overall effort.

For the rest of that day, the Army of the Potomac's actions were very disjointed, and Lee took full advantage of that confusion and re-consolidated his forces. Hooker finally recovered in the late evening, but by that point he had lost his nerve, so he decided to withdraw his army. He made this decision even though Lee was badly over-extended and Hooker's two most aggressive corps commanders, Major Generals John Reynolds and George Meade, were poised to strike with fresh troops who had been held in reserve.[7] Had Hooker properly shared his Commander's Intent with his generals and specified their authorities in his plan, the Union could possibly have defeated Lee decisively and shortened the war by a year or more. The lesson for leaders is simple—don't be like Hooker. Share your vision and designate everyone's authorities.

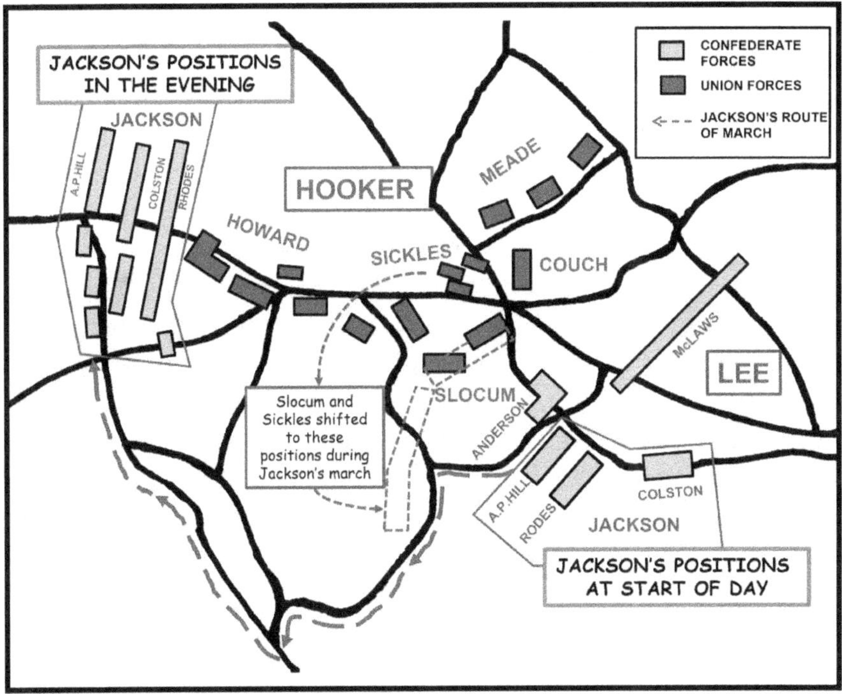

Stonewall Jackson's "left hook" around Chancellorsville wrecks Major General Hooker's battle plan (Adapted from Map by Hal Jespersen, www.cwmaps.com)

DYNAMIC TASKING

The framing process I have described throughout this chapter has an implied assumption that the leader starts the process already knowing the end state. This is certainly ideal for both the leader and the task executor, but in the real world it is not always possible. Fortunately, there is no reason why leaders cannot frame tasks just as effectively in a dynamic environment. They simply have to modify the way they define the task.

In many cases, the leader can clearly envision the final objective, but the end state to achieve it cannot be defined at the outset. In that case, she can employ a conditional framing approach where the task is defined incrementally, using the insights gained at each step to determine the next one. I had to take this approach with our facilities plan at Bagram. A big element of my job was making sure all the Air Force units had the facilities they needed to execute their missions. Space was at a premium and the base was constantly changing configuration as we replaced structures erected randomly at the start of the war with a more rational base design. On one occasion, I had to allocate space for three distinct engineering units, so I pulled in a lieutenant from one unit and a captain from another and tasked them to spend a week and develop some options for how to utilize the real estate and the construction teams to bed down all three organizations.

This may sound like I adopted the Major Nebulus style of leadership, but I assure you I had not. I didn't simply wax poetic and tell them "I'll know what I want when I see it. Good luck!" I gave the two officers specific parameters and priorities for satisfying the needs and wants of each team and they clearly understood the confines of the real estate they had to work within. They also brought personal engineering expertise to the task that allowed them to spot things I might have missed if I had made the final plan all by myself, and I encouraged them to leverage those insights. Unlike my lieutenant friend from years prior who had worked for Major Nebulus, these two officers knew *exactly* what problem they were trying to solve for me. Note that I also specified a formal progress check so I could give them guidance on where to go next, depending upon what we discovered.

At that check, they gave me some very innovative options. They presented seven different courses of actions – or COAs in military-speak—and showed me the advantages and drawbacks of each. After some good discussion, we ended up choosing COA 2 "with a twist," the twist being that I asked them to swap ownership of two minor buildings on their plan. With that decision made, COA 2 with a twist became the ultimate end state for the big task. We then launched the execution phase, which included assembling the remaining buildings and relocating the units. We set milestones & timelines and over the next several weeks, we successfully moved all three units into their new homes.

Leaders who plan to win regularly need to be comfortable with the flexibility required for conditional framing because in many cases, important tasks are to be found on a landscape that is continuously changing. I referenced war plans as a form of framing earlier in the chapter and they are a perfect illustration of how to embed the management of constantly evolving tasks right into the guiding document. Virtually all war plans have clearly stated objectives, with at least an implied ideal end state. However, whatever else they are, battlefields are not static, and every competent tactical commander knows "No plan survives first contact" with the enemy. It is a rare occasion in history when a commander executes a plan exactly as written because the opposing plan is specifically designed to disrupt and defeat it.

Professional military planners account for this by embedding a series of pivot points within the battle plan called **branches and sequels**. Knowing that actual events will quickly deviate from the plan, the planners anticipate likely outcomes that may differ from the original plan. These outcomes may achieve results beyond the desired objectives or fall well short of them. Branches provide guidance for front-line commanders when they need to recover from setbacks, while sequels allow them to reinforce successes as the battle progresses. The whole battle plan is built with the assumption that the conditions will change, so the actions must change and ultimately the end state evolves, too.

When General Eisenhower received his directive for Operation OVERLORD, his superiors added a broad branch and sequel qualifier into the order: "Notwithstanding the target date above you will be prepared at any time to take immediate advantage of favorable circumstances, such as withdrawal by the enemy on your front, to effect a reentry into the Continent with such forces as you have available at the time . . ."[8] Ultimately, Eisenhower was not able to accelerate the invasion date, but once his forces did land in Europe, he empowered his subordinate commanders with the same authority to adjust their task framings when circumstances permitted.

They did this to great effect when it came time to cross the Rhine River into Germany itself. This stage of the operation was critical and was expected to be both challenging and costly, as the armies would have to construct pontoon bridges while under fire. Eisenhower assigned British Field Marshal Bernard Montgomery to lead the advance and Montgomery developed Operation PLUNDER, which called for making the crossings a very deliberate and closely coordinated process by slowly and steadily accruing the mass needed to push across the river along the entire front.

But when the conditions suddenly changed, so did the task execution. Brigadier General William Hoge was in command of the leading element of Lieutenant General Courtney Hodges' 1st Army, and when he arrived at his Rhine River staging point near the town of Remagen on March 7, 1945, he saw something no one expected—the Ludendorff Bridge across the river was still standing, although General Hoge could also see German demolition crews scrambling all over the bridge preparing to blow it. So instead of digging in and waiting for the rest of 1st Army to come up and execute an opposed crossing per the original plan, General Hoge executed a better sequel. He immediately threw combat forces onto the bridge to drive off the

The Ludendorff Bridge across the Rhine River at Remagen (U.S. Army)

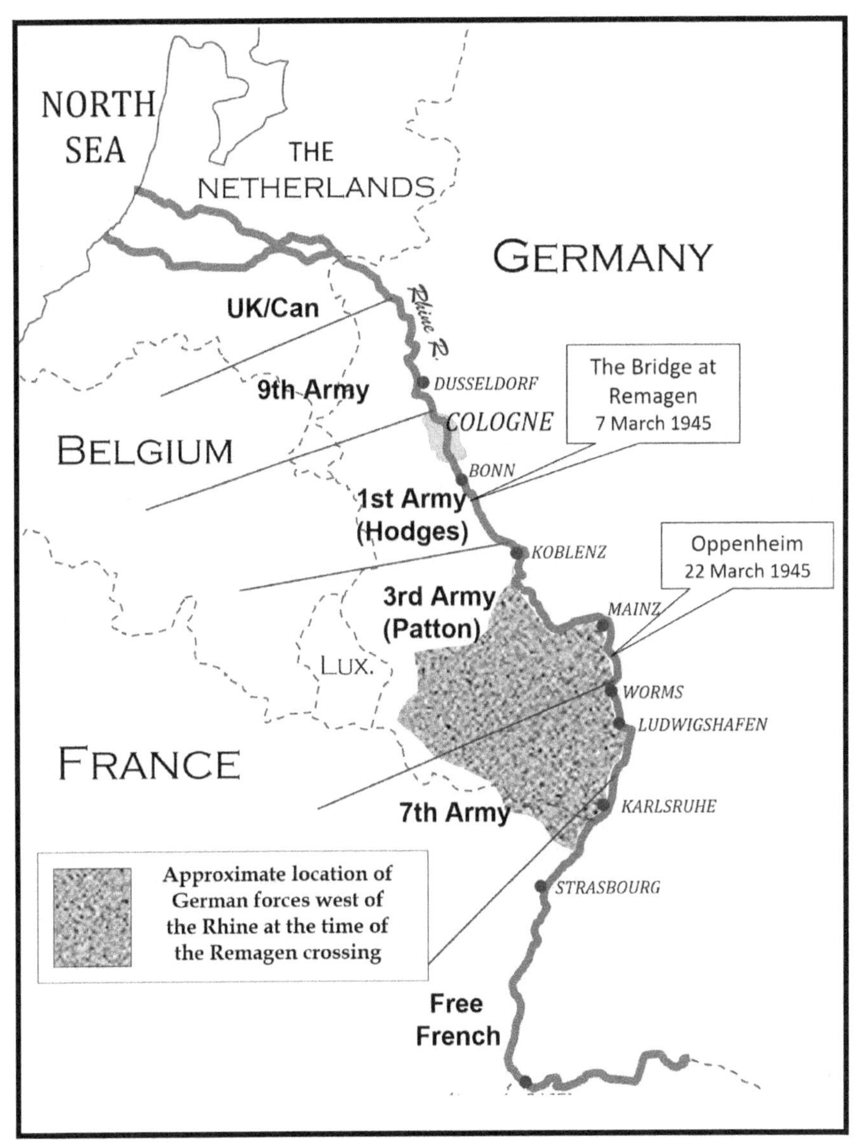

Generals Hodges and Patton accelerate the crossing of the Rhine River (March 1945)

Germans and remove the explosives. The Germans successfully detonated some of their munitions during this battle, which weakened the bridge, but did not destroy it, so follow-on forces continued to rush across the span to secure a position on the German side of the river.

When he came up, General Hodges ordered construction of a tactical steel treadway bridge and a pontoon bridge parallel to the Ludendorff and he used all three structures to get his Army into Germany well ahead of schedule. Meanwhile, Lieutenant General George Patton's 3rd Army was also advancing the timetable in its sector. When Patton arrived at his crossing point at the little town of Oppenheim, he did not think the opposition forces were strong enough to stop him from crossing immediately. So Patton being Patton, he quietly moved forces across the river by small numbers in the darkness of the night of March 22, 1945. Those advance troops were able to establish a secure bridgehead behind which Patton's engineers ran a pontoon bridge across the river. The rest of Patton's army raced into Germany, where they assembled for the final push to end the war well ahead of the PLUNDER timelines. Generals Hoge and Patton both took "immediate advantage of the favorable circumstances" to give Eisenhower a huge windfall that enabled him to accelerate the entire battle plan in Germany and complete the Allied victory just six weeks later.

While the Rhine crossings are an excellent historical example of the judicious use of branches and sequels, the job descriptions for most leaders reading this book probably do not include the conquest of an enemy nation. Fortunately, one need not be a combat commander in a war to use conditional framing, or to employ tools like branches and sequels to manage tasks in a dynamic environment. Here's a hypothetical example of a framing incorporating branches and sequels in a different setting.

Let's suppose Pat is the regional manager for an office-based service company. Pat's Vice President calls to say the company has decided to open a new office in the city of Newville. The VP sends a basic business plan for the new office, including financial goals and a budget and tells Pat to make it happen. Pat runs these numbers, determines the ideal neighborhoods within Newville where the new office could be located, and then breaks the project into two tasks. Pat assigns John to design the staff structure and then hire and train the new employees, using a simple framing with the objective and a series of timelines and milestones. To Mary goes the task of acquiring and outfitting the office space, but this requires a framing with a series of sequential milestones because Mary's final solution will depend upon the outcomes from the proceeding steps. Pat builds flexibility into the framing as follows:

<u>Milestone 1</u>: Within the next 10 days, please gather current rental rates for commercial office space within the neighborhoods of Upper Heights, Old Town Center, and Reynolds Forest (see attached map of Newville)

If the rates in any of these neighborhoods are at least 10% *below* the target rate shown on the accompanying table, then you can disregard Milestones 2 and 3. Instead, place a bid in that neighborhood for whichever available space of approx 5,000 SF you think will serve us best.

If the rates in all of these neighborhoods are at least 20% *above* the target rate, then please take an additional ten days and collect rental rate data for the following neighborhoods, as well, before proceeding to Milestone 2: Lower Heights, Riverside, Parkview, Bluedale and Westend.

Thus, Pat has given Mary a branch plan to follow if the ideal neighborhoods prove to be too pricey and a sequel to pursue that will get the task done faster if the prices are especially favorable. If Mary's research determines the rates are within the expected range, then neither the branch nor sequel will apply and she will simply proceed through the rest of the milestones and lease an office based on the outcomes of all these actions.

Dynamic tasking can work equally well for any type of mission, and leaders should be ready to incorporate such flexibility into their framings, *but only when it makes sense to do so.* That is, if a straight-forward framing with an unambiguous end state will do the trick, there is no good reason to add unnecessary complexity to the task. And whatever scheme the leader chooses to use to convey the task, he must never forget the framing's customer is the task executor and the framing's sole purpose is to enable mission accomplishment. A person equipped with a complete and coherent framing holds a roadmap to victory, and the leader who provides one is therefore Leading to Win.

Case Study: The Messiah Frames it Up

"And to the ends of the earth . . ."

Jesus Christ of Nazareth claimed to be the messiah, that is, the promised deliverer of the Jewish nation prophesied in the Hebrew scriptures we today call the Old Testament. We might therefore presume that Jesus' objective statement would be pretty big in its ambitions and its significance, and as we will see, he does not disappoint. According to the Bible, Jesus himself had to fulfill a special mission that came directly from God, which was to die as a sacrifice to cleanse all of humanity's sin. But his death on the cross only makes individual people *eligible* for salvation; to claim it, each person must choose to make a pledge of faith in the resurrected Messiah.[*] Jesus needed a plan to enable as many people as possible to make that pledge, and this became the mission he passed to his followers.

In order for Jesus' sacrificial death to have the requisite meaning, he spent most of his three-year ministry executing two tasks God had assigned to him. The first was to educate the Jewish nation about the true nature of the Kingdom of God and to convince them he was the Messiah. The second was to play a leadership role for a small group

---

[*] This concept is encapsulated in one of the most famous verses in the Bible, John 3:16, "For God so loved the world, that He gave His only Son, that whoever believes in Him should not perish but have eternal life."

of people who would carry on after his ascension back to God. If all of humanity was to be saved through his name, then all of humanity would have to *know* his name and his teachings. Jesus' big objective, then—the goal he needed his team to achieve—was to spread the Word as far and wide as possible.

Jesus didn't use a one-page framing or an operational order to summarize the objective. Instead, in the last moments before he departed from his apostles for the final time, he simply told them what they must do: "Therefore go and make disciples of all nations, baptizing them in the name of the Father and of the Son and of the Holy Spirit, and teaching them to obey everything I have commanded you."[9] Although just a single sentence, this "Great Commission" from Jesus is an incredibly effective example of an ideal objective statement. The task is to *make disciples*, and Jesus also gave the apostles three specific sub-tasks:

- *Go*
- *Baptize* in the name of the Trinity
- *Teach* Jesus' lessons for godly living

Moreover, Jesus made it clear this objective has no limits in terms of the scope of the target audience, for the disciples must be from *all nations*. And just to be sure the apostles had no doubt what he meant, Jesus said this in another passage describing these final instructions: "You will be my witnesses in Jerusalem, and in all Judea and Samaria, and *to the ends of the earth*."[10]

This may well be the most expansive tasking in all history. Only when all the world's people know the whole Gospel and commit themselves to Jesus will this job be done. Moreover, because there will be uncounted future generations of people to reach, the objective is unlimited in time, too. Clearly, this mission could not be accomplished by a mere dozen people, and that is the whole point of his objective. Because Jesus' vision of mission accomplishment required nothing less than the redemption of all humanity, those whom Jesus was tasking were really being told to establish an open-ended mechanism to ensure that all people in all places and all centuries can know him. Today we call this mechanism the Christian Church.

One can imagine our own first reaction to such a tasking would be something along the lines of "Sure, Lord, we'll get right on that . . ." Fortunately for the apostles, Jesus knew the task was daunting, so he gave them a starting place and time for their mission: "Do not leave Jerusalem, but wait for the gift my Father promised, which you have heard me speak about. For John baptized with water, but *in a few days* you will be baptized with the Holy Spirit."[11] So the team's first and only milestone & timeline was to wait patiently for a few days until God provided a resource for their mission.

That resource—the Holy Spirit—would prove invaluable because it gave the apostles the guidance, the knowledge, and the strength they needed for the challenges ahead. Jesus had told his followers to be patient for they would soon be "clothed with power from on high."[12] They obeyed, and their patience was indeed rewarded in short order:

When the day of Pentecost came, they were all together in one place. Suddenly a sound like the blowing of a violent wind came from heaven and filled the whole house where they were sitting. They saw what seemed to be tongues of fire that separated and came to rest on each of them. All of them were all filled with the Holy Spirit and began to speak in other tongues as the Spirit enabled them.[13]

The apostles were now equipped to win. Indeed, the Holy Spirit transformed the Apostle Peter into such an eloquent orator that his impromptu sermon about the messiah won him more than 3,000 converts on the spot.[14] Not bad for a rustic fisherman's first day on the task.

Finally, Jesus even clarified the range of the apostles' authority while executing their mission, and like every other part of this program, it was colossal. "If you forgive anyone's sins, their sins are forgiven; if you do not forgive them, they are not forgiven."[15] Jesus had essentially delegated his own authorities to the apostles, and so they were fully armed with the means and the confidence to move forward with the Great Commission. And so they did, for nearly 2,000 years later, Jesus' on-going task is as vigorous as ever, delivering positive results every day, all over the globe. Jesus' mastery in framing the task for his team was certainly a key contributor to success, and it can be just as powerful a tool for any leader.

BUILDING A DEEP BENCH

Principle #2: Know Your People

&

Principle #3: Hire for Quality

I had been working for Colonel Monti for some time when he asked me to take on the reorganization project I described in Chapter 1. While I had been using that time to glean as much wisdom as I could from one of the best mentors I ever had, he was using the time to take his measure of me. When he decided to re-shape his division, he determined I was the right officer to tackle this project because he felt confident I would be able to assemble the kind of plan he envisioned. This confidence turned out to be well-placed because as I mentioned earlier, Chief Khoma and I delivered a big win for Colonel Monti's team. In retrospect, this is all somewhat ironic *because the Air Force never intended me to be a part of his team at all.*

I was originally assigned to Randolph Air Force Base to be the Logistics Support Officer on the headquarters staff of 19th Air Force, which was an organization responsible for all flying training in the Air Force. Once I was in place, however, it was obvious this head-quarters did not really need a Logistics Support Officer as a full-time position, and I found myself with little to do on most days. My boss was Colonel Rick Bereit, and he recognized that I was not getting the experience the assignment was supposed to provide. More importantly, he realized I could also be of value elsewhere, and so he offered my services on a part-time basis to a colleague across the base who often commented he needed an additional action officer on his team. That colleague was Virgil Monti, who was initially suspicious about this offer of "free manpower" because it was so unusual.

Colonel Bereit assured him there was no hidden agenda, so Colonel Monti agreed to take me on as an unofficial member of the Logistics Plans Division, working half of each day with his team. Over the next several months, he asked me to assist a couple of his permanent staff with their projects and thus had the opportunity to gauge my skills and abilities. Meanwhile, I was getting the opportunity to learn some completely new aspects of the Air Force's logistics enterprise and to broaden my network as I worked with more and more people on the Air Education and Training Command staff.

About six months into this part-time gig, Colonel Monti asked me out of the blue, "When are you going to come over here permanently?"

Taken completely by surprise by the question, I stammered, "I didn't even know that was an option."

He went on, "I have a position coming open I need to fill and I have a program I think you'd be ideal for, but you couldn't do this unless you were here full-time and assigned to our director's staff."

Colonel Virgil Monti

I recovered quickly and assured him I was definitely interested in the offer. A few short weeks later, after some negotiations with 19th Air Force leadership, I had my reassignment orders in hand and I formally reported in as the newest staff member of the Logistics Plans Division. Up to this point Colonel Monti had not explained what he had in mind for me, nor had I asked, but once I was officially on his team he said, "I want you to be the lead planning officer preparing Altus Air Force Base, Oklahoma, to receive a squadron of the new C-17 cargo aircraft that will be based there for training aircrews."

I was thrilled at the prospect and fully agreed with Colonel Monti that it was a perfect fit for me. He had few other people with any significant background in airlift operations and he had discerned my passion for that mission, so I was highly qualified to manage the kinds of issues this project would spawn. He also recognized that I could "herd the cats" effectively, which was critical in this case because there were so many moving pieces. Additionally, he had seen me collaborate effectively with other staff members across the directorate during my temporary status, and he recognized that would be a key skill for whomever was running this program. Finally, I suspect he saw that I was a confident communicator, even when addressing a senior audience, which was important because he needed someone he could rely on to draft persuasive point papers and provide useful analysis at staff meetings where this project was the topic of discussion.

The C-17 Globemaster III (U.S. Air Force)

Looking back on it now it is clear to me that in spite of his initial hesitation to bring me over part-time, Colonel Monti viewed the arrangement right from the beginning as a sort of internship for me and a grand opportunity for him to really get to know me. The more he learned, the more certain he became that I was just who he needed to bed down the C-17s. Over time, my duties spun off into other programs and eventually I was given the reorganization task. My professional growth during the two years I worked for Colonel Monti was tremendous and my accomplishments were significant, too, but none of it would have happened if I hadn't been working for a leader who made it a priority to know his people.

Leading to Win requires a pool of capable people to take on important tasks, and the bigger the pool and the more capabilities each member brings to the table, the better the prospects for winning at any task. However, leaders will not be able to employ this pool of talent to maximum benefit if they haven't first invested in getting to know their people. This principle may at first appear to be so obvious that it does not warrant a deep discussion. After all, it's axiomatic that all good leaders should know their people, right? Well, it certainly ought to be, but this is another one of those concepts that means different things to different people.

I will characterize this principle in terms that directly relate to the unique definition of great leadership laid out in Chapter 2, that is, the ability of a leader to get the job done right. Specifically for the purposes of this book, Principle #2 above—know your people—describes an analytical process that informs a leader about the attributes and aptitudes of each member of the team. This process requires leaders to intentionally commit themselves to gathering all the insights they can about their team members' capabilities and limitations, for it is the sum total of these insights that builds a "deep bench" of skilled team members ready to accomplish important missions.

* * *

Colonel Monti had a unique opportunity to get to know me and profile my strengths and gaps, and he took full advantage of it. However, most leaders don't have the luxury of studying a no-strings-attached team member for several months as their means to get to know someone. A leader seeking to know his people often takes the time to develop extensive personal knowledge about each team member first—their work history, where they grew up, their education, their family, their career aspirations, and so forth. While this does not exactly fit the definition of "knowing your people" I put forward above, it is still a valid approach.

Many leaders will argue they must learn such personal details before they can form accurate professional assessments about their team members, and I find this to be a very persuasive argument for which I offer no criticism. Within this phase of the Leading to Win model, my advice to each leader is to adopt whatever style works best to get to know her people, provided it generates the knowledge needed to make wise task assignments. However, I'd also caution all leaders to beware of a common trap: never assume a style focused on personal knowledge will *automatically* produce the needed understanding of task-specific capabilities. Achieving the kind of knowledge necessary for great leadership ultimately requires its own effort, so I will offer some suggestions, observations, and examples in this chapter that may help with this activity.

FACE-TO-FACE STRATEGIES

Whatever methodology a leader uses to get to know her people, it must include the leader actually *spending time* with those people. The work environment often dictates whether this will be easy and natural or will require intentional planning. My first role as an Air Force officer, for instance, was Vehicle Management Officer for the 7th Mobile Aerial Port Squadron at McChord Air Force Base, Washington. I led a small team of people who all worked in and around the same physical space. Our duties ensured we interacted with one another on a daily basis. In that situation, getting to know my whole team on a personal level and to see their strengths and gaps firsthand was an easy thing and it happened quite naturally.

As I rose to positions overseeing larger and more geographically dispersed organizations, however, I could no longer rely on such a casual approach if I really wanted to get to know my people. When I reached that stage in my career, I made it a priority to deliberately allocate time to my key subordinates so I could learn about who they were and what they could do. When I took command of the transportation squadron at Scott Air Force Base, Illinois, in 1999, I experimented with a proactive scheduling process I had been imagining for some time. It worked so well that I continued it throughout the rest of my career.

I started by blocking on my calendar a recurring meeting time with each of my key team members. This in and of itself was not terribly innovative, because almost all leaders schedule one-on-one time with their subordinates. My innovation was the way I executed these meetings. As a young officer I had been disappointed that I didn't see my commanders in the work centers more often. Once in command myself, I discovered how little free time I had for random visits with my people, so I made it standard practice to always travel to their work centers for the meetings. Once there, I usually reserved the first few minutes of our time to exchange updates on key open items like any other recurring check-in, but the rest of the visit—and the agenda—belonged to the host.

I wanted my key people to own these engagements and to use them to make me smarter about their operations. This also gave me the chance to spend time with their teams, and to make me aware of the most important issues they were working at their level. In every unit where I did this, my teams gave me positive feedback about how much they valued these sessions, and the process was equally valuable for me.

This construct kept me up-to-date on what was happening within my organization and it also allowed me to dedicate time within a busy schedule to examine each member of my team more closely. Which issues each leader identified and how they presented them told me loads about their potential to handle complex problems. The visits and the interaction with their teams also helped me gauge how well their people were responding to their leadership. It did not take long before I had an accurate profile of my team members' skills and personalities.

As a more senior officer, I also developed a formal mentoring program for my junior officers. I held seminars where I would present topics aimed at making them better leaders within the Air Force. Sometimes these were very practical lessons such as how to write a quality medal citation or the things to consider when applying for a new assignment. In other sessions we talked about broader topics such as leadership styles and military ethics. The questions they asked, the opinions they offered, and the changes I saw—or didn't see—in their work after these sessions again helped me to get to really know them and recognize the tasks they would or would not be able to accomplish well.

Work center visits and group meetings are helpful vehicles when a leader is trying to get to know his people, but nothing is better than watching those people in action, as they demonstrate specific skills the leader is trying to evaluate. Sports coaches, for instance, use try-outs to determine who to draft, and pre-season scrimmages to decide who to start in the regular season games. Within the military, exercises serve a similar purpose, and they can be a useful "crucible" where people soar or crash under the pressure of new and unfamiliar scenarios. Leaders can then use these observations to decide who can fill key roles in real-world operations.

I watched this dynamic unfold during a series of exercises we held at Charleston Air Force Base in preparation for our Operational Readiness Inspection (ORI). ORIs are make-or-break events because a poor grade essentially calls into question the wing's ability to perform its combat mission, and it quite often costs the Wing Commander his or her job, too! The preparatory exercises, however, are learning events, and we use them to identify and correct any mistakes we observe, with no harm done. Some people flourish under the challenge and receive positive attention when senior leaders see their skills and abilities driving mission accomplishment. On the other hand, some folks in significant roles don't handle the responsibilities well at all.

In this case that is exactly what happened to our Chief of Plans, the lieutenant colonel who was directly responsible for managing the exercise process. His oversight of the series of exercises leading up to the ORI was essentially a trial by fire that would validate his readiness for executive level roles. To be blunt, he failed the trial, and did so in short order. The wing leadership responded boldly, agreeing this officer didn't have what it takes to produce positive outcomes at that level and so he couldn't remain in the Chief of Plans role with the ORI looming on the horizon. The wing commander therefore reassigned him to regular flying duties and called in a new leader who immediately brought positive energy and better direction to the exercise process. In the end our wing scored an EXCELLENT rating on the ORI, at least in part because the wing leadership took the time to get to know who had the skills to deliver positive outcomes and who did not.

STRENGTHS, GAPS AND WEAKNESSES

In Chapter 2, I specifically commented that "developing" tomorrow's leaders must not be the priority of a great leader, but I also indicated I had observed that such development often goes hand-in-hand with great leadership that is focused on getting today's job done by assigning the right people to the right task. The time for explaining that relationship has arrived.

The whole point of the Know Your People principle is to create a mental inventory of team members' unique skills. A person with the skill to perform a certain element of a task well can be said to have a **strength** in that area. This definition is intentionally vague because there are an almost unlimited number of strengths a leader can evaluate and assign. A person can have top-notch analytical skills, she could be an especially gifted communicator, or he may display uncanny empathy with others. Two seemingly opposing traits may even both be strengths for different people. For instance, one person may be especially adept at detailed planning, while someone else seems to thrive best in a chaotic, unscripted situation. Obviously, these two people will be most likely to succeed when they are assigned tasks that call for the trait that is a strength for them.

To make sure the right match happens, each leader must be just as certain about the skills his people do *not* possess as he is about the strengths they do have. Earlier in the chapter I referred to the absence of a skill as a **gap**. Cataloguing each member's strengths and gaps is fundamental to knowing the people on a team, but it is not the end of the process unless that leader wants to live in a reality where their teams' abilities are fixed and permanent. As this version of reality severely limits the leader's ability to win, it is not one I would recommend. Fortunately, it is not a reality leaders need to accept, either, because a critical part of the process of knowing their people is taking steps to convert gaps into strengths whenever possible.

Once a leader has a solid grasp of her subordinates' proven abilities, she must then determine what other skills they have the *potential* to master. These are the gaps that are actually candidates for development, and the leader who fails to invest in those opportunities is limiting the long-term achievements of his people. Moreover, that leader is also limiting his own success because the more gaps a leader accepts within his team, the less likely he'll have a person available with the right skills to accomplish a demanding mission. When a leader identifies a trait that needs improvement in a subordinate, he should do whatever he can to enable the improvement.

In many cases, some formal training is the only thing necessary to bridge the gap. That was my rationale for holding the officer mentoring session I mentioned above about writing quality citations for medal recommendations. My officers were consistently sending me poorly drafted citations, which generated considerable rework at multiple levels and slowed the process of recognizing our Airmen for the great work they did. This came about not because the officers had bad writing skills, but because no one had ever explained to them what a "good" citation text should look like. I conducted a one-hour lesson on the topic during which I pointed out some of the common mistakes I was seeing and I gave them some guidelines for better structure. The quality of their drafts immediately improved; for all intents and purposes, that performance gap ceased to exist.

In other cases, building a skill may call for an individualized approach that takes more time and effort. A leader can *stretch* a subordinate by assigning a task outside the subordinate's comfort zone and appointing someone with the right skill to help coach the learner through the task. Many people will embrace the challenge, accomplish the task, and enhance their competence for the target skill as a result. None of this is rocket science and most good leaders are already doing similar things. I emphasize the process here primarily to demonstrate that the development of specific skills for budding leaders is a fundamental element of knowing their people and is an enabler for Leading to Win. For a textbook example of this from military history, we can look at what I call the "Saga of the Stretching of Phil Sheridan" . . .

Philip H. Sheridan graduated from West Point in 1853 as an infantry officer and spent the first several years of his service administering "Indian policy" in Oregon and the Washington Territory. He worked with horses, but only as a means of transportation for his troops. Sheridan gained a solid reputation during these assignments and when the Civil War broke out in 1861, he headed east to join the action there. General Henry Halleck was commanding Western forces from St Louis at the time Sheridan passed through that city, so Halleck scooped him up and started the stretching process. Halleck appointed then-Captain Sheridan to be president of a board of officers charged with auditing the disbursement accounts for Halleck's department.[16] Sheridan performed this task very well, and as a result Halleck assigned him to be the Quartermaster *and* Commissary Officer for Major General Samuel Curtis' Army of Southwest Missouri. Sheridan gave invaluable support to Curtis in this role, delivering critical supplies and food from distant depots. Sheridan's reliable logistics enabled Curtis to fight and win the little-known, but strategically significant, Battle of Pea Ridge in Arkansas. Following this battle, Sheridan was ready for the next challenge, and it came from an unexpected quarter. Austin Blair, the governor of Michigan, was visiting his troops and also looking for a regular officer to command his newly formed 2nd Michigan Cavalry Regiment. Governor Blair became acquainted with Captain Sheridan and decided he had found his man. Sheridan accepted the offer and went right to work "dressed in a coat and trousers of captain of infantry, but recast as a colonel of cavalry . . ."[17]

Major General Philip Sheridan
(Library of Congress)

Sheridan had never even served in, much less commanded, cavalry forces before, so this truly was a stretch for him, as was the immediate leap in rank from captain to colonel. It was also an ideal testing ground. Although a Civil War regiment was a respectable unit in terms of size and importance, it was still far enough down the organizational chart that if Sheridan had been ineffective in his new role, it would not have made an out-sized impact on the Army as a whole. As it turned out, though, Sheridan proved very effective and soon won a reputation for cavalry operations that was just as good as the one he had earned for infantry and quartermaster duties. He was quickly advanced upward, commanding divisions with great distinction in two different armies in the west. Major General Ulysses Grant saw Sheridan in action during the Chattanooga campaign, and he apparently liked what he saw. When Grant went east to command all Union forces, he brought Sheridan with him and assigned him as the new cavalry corps commander in the Army of the Potomac. Grant probably would not have made this kind of appointment if Sheridan had not proven himself in the stretch role with the 2nd Michigan.

Prior to Sheridan's arrival in Virginia, the Union cavalry arm there had achieved little of note, while Robert E. Lee's Confederate cavalry under the flamboyant Major General Jeb Stuart had ranged freely and given the federal forces endless headaches. Sheridan believed he could change that, but he quickly ran afoul of his new commander, Major General George Meade. Sheridan stated, "The acrimonious interview ended . . . and he [Meade] went to General Grant's headquarters and repeated the conversation to him, mentioning that I had said I could whip Stuart. At this General Grant remarked: 'Did he say so? Then let him go out and do it.' This intimation was immediately acted upon by General Meade."[18]

Sheridan proved to be as good as his word. He amassed his cavalry and went after Stuart's forces relentlessly, ultimately killing Stuart himself at the Battle of Yellow Tavern in 1864. Sheridan's troopers then laid waste to a critical railroad line between Lee and his supply base in the city of Richmond and destroyed a series of Confederate sub-depots. Sheridan had effectively flipped the script on cavalry operations in Virginia and from that point on, the Union cavalry held the upper hand.

Sheridan proved himself again during the Shenandoah campaign of 1864-65, when Grant elevated him further. Grant created the independent Army of the Shenandoah and gave it to Sheridan, who chased down and eliminated Confederate General Jubal Early's army and fulfilled Grant's orders to turn "the Shenandoah Valley [into] a barren waste . . . so that crows flying over it for the balance of the season will have to carry their provender with them."[19] Sheridan returned from the Shenandoah just in time to help force the surrender of the Confederate forces in Virginia by leading important actions during the Battle of the Five Forks, the destruction of Richard Ewell's corps, and the final envelopment of Lee's Army.

Though lesser known than many of the other figures of the Civil War such as Grant, Lee, Sherman, or Jackson, Sheridan's accomplishments during that conflict were just as significant and he was arguably among the top echelon of military leaders ultimately responsible for the Union victory. He was able to make these contributions because his superiors saw his potential early and continuously stretched his skill sets. Leaders who want to be able to achieve great things with their team should be on the lookout for the next Phil Sheridan, and when they spot one, they should find stretch opportunities to convert gaps into strengths.

At some point, however, leaders must determine whether a missing skill is a gap that can be filled or a true **weakness**, that is, a skill the person will simply never master. In recent years, it has become unfashionable to use the term "weakness" because of its negative connotation, but I disagree with this philosophy. Acknowledging a weakness should not be equated with failure. *Everyone* has certain things they are just not suited to do well, no matter how much they wish they were or how hard they are willing to work at it. When that is the case, both the leader and the subordinate should recognize those weaknesses, and then spend time on other shortcomings where there is a real possibility of improvement. Remember, Leading to Win is about matching the right person to the right task, not about trying to create a fantasy world where everyone can do every task. Once a leader has stretched her team to its reasonable limits, she should be ready to fully and honestly catalog everyone's strengths and weaknesses. At that point leaders know their people.

GEORGE MARSHALL: MASTER AT WORK

General of the Army George Marshall is a perfect historical example of a leader who made it a priority to know his people and build a deep bench. Marshall was the first of only four World War II era Army officers to wear five stars and he served as Army Chief of Staff and

Chairman of the Joint Chiefs of Staff for the entire war. President Franklin Roosevelt considered Marshall indispensable, and he was so instrumental to the successful prosecution of the war that he became known as the "Organizer of Victory." In that role, one of Marshall's most important responsibilities was assigning senior Army officers to key commands and positions all over the world, a job he did consistently well. His success rate in this arena did not happen by mere chance, but because he had been preparing for this mission for years.

A decade before he came to Washington as the Chief of Staff, he spent five years in charge

General of the Army George Marshall
(U.S. Army)

of training and curriculum at the Infantry School at Fort Benning, Georgia. Nearly every future senior leader in the Army passed through the course during Marshall's tenure there, so he observed, tested, and interacted with all of them as they tackled the school's challenges and exercises. Marshall began composing what he called "my little black book." This was a collection of notes on all the officers he taught at Benning, compiled for "future reference." [20] He also tracked the career progression of the most impressive officers as they rose through the ranks and sometimes used his growing influence to intervene in the assignment system to put them in positions where they could enhance a skill or fill a gap in experience.

By the time he became Chief of Staff on September 1, 1939—the very same day Hitler invaded Poland to start the European war—he had a homemade *Who's Who* of the Army's senior officers in his desk drawer. Marshall invested his prime years getting to know his people and then he applied that knowledge to the great advantage of the Allies. "When in 1940 and 1941 the Chief of Staff looked for division and corps commanders, he knew intimately scores of officers who had worked with him at Benning and who valued the same essentials of battle leadership."[21] Among his special protégés were an instructor he supervised at the Infantry School named Omar Bradley and a then-Lieutenant Colonel named Dwight Eisenhower, both of whom would eventually join him in the five-star club after he put them in critical commands throughout the course of the war.[*]

Marshall's inspiration to evaluate a whole generation of officers was obviously critical to his ability to build winning teams during the war, but that was only half the reason for his success. He also understood there is a complementary aspect to the process that successful leaders must acknowledge and own. In Chapter 2, I listed several actions a leader must take to develop the succeeding generation of leaders and the final step was:

Assess everyone's long-term prospects and make sure the leaders with the highest potential stand out

---

[*] The fourth Army 5-star was General Douglas MacArthur, who was far senior to every other general in the Army at the war's start, although President Roosevelt awarded Marshall his 5th star a day *before* MacArthur to remove any doubt about who was #1 in the Army! General Hap Arnold of the Army Air Force also became a 5-star. He is considered the Air Force's only 5-star even though he was technically an Army officer at the time of his promotion because the U.S. Air Force didn't become an independent service until 1947.

An honest assessment process includes facing the unpleasant reality that some candidates for future leadership simply do not have what it takes and likely never will. When a leader's assessment of a subordinate's skill set produces an unfavorable ratio of confirmed weaknesses relative to strengths, it is incumbent upon the leader to steer that person into a more appropriate career path which may not even be in the same organization or career field. In addition to lauding Marshall's conduct of the war, historians also commend him for his decision to remove a lot of aging officers from the Army once he became Chief of Staff. Marshall knew these officers would not be up to the task of commanding troops in a world war, so in the two years leading up to Pearl Harbor, he retired scores of them—especially at the senior level—in order to create promotion opportunities for all those younger officers he was convinced could produce victories on the battlefield.[22]

George McClellan: Wrong Man for the Job

When done proactively, as Marshall did during his housecleaning of the Army, the individual in question will be sidelined before he is in a position to prove the leader's negative opinion right. It's a thorny proposition to claim mission accomplishment happened because someone was *exempted* from a task and as a result, historical examples "proving the negative" are hard to come by. On the other hand, history does provide instances where a leader does not recognize a person's weaknesses in time to prevent them causing significant harm to a mission. A good example of this is the on-again, off-again relationship between President Abraham Lincoln and Major General George McClellan . . .

When the Civil War began, Lincoln had just ascended to the presidency and knew very little about any of the rising generation of military leaders he would need to call upon to win the war. He had very senior veterans like Winfield Scott and Henry Halleck to guide him initially, but as time went on, Lincoln would eventually form his own opinions about whom to trust with the most important commands during the war. Nowhere was this learning process more painful than finding a reliable leader for the Army of the Potomac, the Union's most important field unit in the East and the main foil to Robert E. Lee's Army of Northern Virginia.

After the thrashing the Union suffered at the First Battle of Bull Run in July 1861, Lincoln turned to a young officer who seemed to embody both the talent and the energy needed to lead the Union to victory, 34-year old George B. McClellan. A West Pointer, McClellan had served with distinction in the Mexican War, and then left the Army to work as a railroad executive. He was recruited back into the federal army in 1861 as a major general. McClellan was given the task of rebuilding the broken Union forces and there is nearly unanimous agreement that he did a magnificent job of this, because the task required just the sort of administrative and managerial skills he possessed in spades. In fact, history has dubbed him "The Great Organizer" for his work during this period.

The newly minted Army of the Potomac was McClellan's creation and he was its initial commander. However, McClellan proved much more proficient at building the army than *using* that army to attack and destroy the enemy forces opposing him. Although the Army of the Potomac was greatly superior in numbers to its Confederate counterpart, richly equipped and supplied, and at a new high in morale, McClellan repeatedly dithered. He imagined himself to be outnumbered and he always wanted more time for preparations to make sure everything would be perfectly arranged before taking aggressive action. Every order, plea or remonstrance that Lincoln issued to McClellan to get moving was met with a list of reasons why this was not possible.

On those occasions when he did engage the enemy, it was half-heartedly, almost as if his object was to keep his army free from harm rather than employ it to crush the enemy. During the Peninsular Campaign of 1862, McClellan had a real opportunity to overwhelm and annihilate the Army of Northern Virginia, which might have put the Confederacy out of business much sooner. If he had pressed this opportunity, McClellan may have landed in the pantheon of the greatest military leaders in American history. Instead, he yielded the initiative to Lee, who out-foxed him at almost every turn. When this phase of the fighting was complete, both armies were battered, but still whole, and the chance for either to win a quick and decisive victory had passed. Frustrated with McClellan's failure to use the Army offensively as directed and with McClellan's failure to show proper deference to his short chain of command, Lincoln relieved him and gave the Army to Major General John Pope.

Shortly thereafter Pope was ignominiously swept from the field at Second Bull Run and the Army of the Potomac was so wrecked psychologically that Lee took the bold step of invading the North. Lee marched into Maryland, where he hoped to induce that state to join the Confederacy. Lincoln turned back to McClellan again, giving him a second opportunity to rebuild the Army of the Potomac and lead it to victory. Helped by the discovery of the Confederate battle plan when the two armies were facing off around Sharpsburg, Maryland, in September 1862, McClellan did in fact achieve a tactical victory at Antietam. He drove the Confederates back below the Mason-Dixon Line, but again missed the chance to finish off Lee's army.

After more than 23,000 casualties on one of the bloodiest days in American military history, it is hard to argue that McClellan pulled his army's punches at Antietam, but it is indisputable that he failed to follow-up the victory with a vigorous pursuit of Lee's outnumbered and badly mauled army. Instead, McClellan allowed Lee to return to Virginia and then called himself a "savior" for driving the Confederates back to their own territory. Lincoln's main rationale for fighting the war was to end the notion that the Confederacy was a separate nation with its own territory, so McClellan's statement must have galled the President horribly.

President Abraham Lincoln confers with Major General George McClellan shortly before the Battle of Antietam. These two leaders had a stormy relationship. (Library of Congress)

Nonetheless, Lincoln still gave McClellan the

benefit of the doubt and yet *another* opportunity to redeem himself, ordering him to "cross the Potomac and give battle to the enemy or drive him south. Your army must move now, while the roads are good."[23] McClellan responded with plodding movements, more excuses and more insubordination, so Lincoln at last concluded McClellan would never have the ability to lead the Army in the manner he believed was necessary for victory. Lincoln relieved McClellan for good in November 1862, and McClellan soon left the Army altogether.

Had Lincoln been given the opportunity to really know McClellan in the way an effective leader should know his subordinates before assigning them a critical task, he probably wouldn't have appointed McClellan to be the Union's Commanding General. Armed with a better assessment of McClellan, Lincoln might have been able to assign him to a position that maximized the young general's real talents for organization, administration, and morale-building, while keeping him away from a major field command, which McClellan clearly did not have the right temperament or skills to lead successfully.

THE POWER OF CUSTOM FRAMING

Knowing one's people well offers leaders synergies with the framing concept discussed in the previous chapter. A leader who truly knows his people can tailor the framing documents to drive better results. Writing a generic framing with no specific recipient in mind can still produce an effective tasking document, but a customized framing can be even more powerful, and I saw that first-hand when issuing one of my framing documents at Charleston Air Force Base.

I assigned an officer to lead one of the big projects because I knew he brought the necessary technical expertise and attention to detail required to achieve this particular project's goals. I also knew this officer took great pride in his professional reputation and yearned for opportunities to enhance it. I took all of these insights into account when I wrote the framing document. I specifically emphasized the high-level visibility the project would receive from around the Wing, context I would not have included at all if I had not been writing the document specifically *for him.* My goal was to motivate my lieutenant to go the extra mile to accomplish the mission, and it worked. He delivered results beyond my best hopes, and I made sure he received the public credit he was promised. On that occasion I reaped real benefits by framing the task to a personality, a connection good leaders have been making throughout history. Here's a great anecdote from WWII that demonstrates the same concept when the stakes were very high . . .

In June 1942, Admiral Raymond Spruance became a household name after his carrier task force sank four Japanese carriers in the two-day Battle of Midway, a victory that completely turned the course of the Pacific War. After Midway, Spruance was assigned as the Commander of Fifth Fleet. In this position, he and his "Air Boss," Vice Admiral Marc Mitscher, plowed across the Pacific, taking islands and destroying Japanese ships and aircraft every chance they got. After a couple of years of this, the Japanese Navy had been so badly decimated that only one significant surface ship remained afloat—the enormous battleship *Yamato*—and Spruance and Mitscher wanted her dead, too. On April 7, 1945, American reconnaissance aircraft finally spotted the *Yamato* and quickly reported her location.

Spruance's new Chief of Staff, Rear Admiral Arthur C. Davis took the report and drafted a lengthy operational order for attacking the battleship. In *The Fleet at Flood Tide*, historian James D. Hornfischer describes what happened when Davis brought the order to Spruance for signature. "Spruance gave the plan the courtesy of a glance, then, saying nothing, tore it to pieces. He grabbed a piece of paper and scribbled four words, 'Mitsch, you get 'em,' and with a glint in his eye, handed that order back to Davis. 'Art,' Spruance said, 'Mitsch would never forgive me and would think that I was surely slipping if we gave him such a detailed order. He knows what to do.'"[24] And so Mitsch did. He launched more than 300 aircraft to attack the *Yamato* and by mid-afternoon, she was lying on the floor of the Pacific. Mission accomplished!

Spruance's leadership was superb here. He knew his deputy very well because the two admirals had been working, sailing and fighting together for over two years. Specifically, Spruance knew:

1. Mitscher had a very aggressive personality in terms of his approach to battle
2. Mitscher was a proven tactical expert managing air power
3. Mitscher delivered the best results when he was free to manage his own operations

Spruance therefore recognized that the operational plan his staff had prepared would do more harm than good. Instead of motivating Mitscher and his fliers to go "get 'em," the detailed plan would have likely annoyed them, and who does their best work when they are annoyed? Mitscher no doubt smiled broadly when he got Spruance's note, and because he knew he had Spruance's full confidence to get this job done, he would have pulled out all the stops to prove that confidence was well-earned. Spruance's four-word framing document and his intimate knowledge of his deputy doomed the *Yamato*.

Admirals Raymond Spruance (left), Marc Mitscher (2nd from left)
and Arthur Davis (far right) with their boss, Admiral Chester Nimitz
(U.S. Naval History and Heritage Command)

On the other hand, I can't help but wonder if Lee's confusing "take the hill" order at Gettysburg that we discussed in Chapter 3 was the result of this frame-the-task-to-match-your-people dynamic that just went awry. My personal theory is that Lee phrased his order as he did specifically because he was sending it to Ewell. Lee knew that Ewell was new to command at corps level and so Lee may have been concerned that Ewell would be overwhelmed with the expanded responsibilities he was facing. This confidence crisis would be magnified if Ewell—who had been promoted into Stonewall Jackson's former position—also felt like everything he did would be measured against Jackson's near-mythical reputation. If Lee had this sense, then he may have added "if practicable" to his order as a signal to Ewell that Lee trusted him to

General Robert E. Lee
(Library of Congress)

make his own battlefield decision instead of trying to emulate what he thought Jackson would do. In other words, Lee wanted Ewell to feel validated in his new position, which would give him the confidence he needed to try to take the hill.

However, there were a couple of things Lee apparently did not consider. First, Lee had formed the habit of issuing his orders to Jackson with wide latitude or in the form of a suggestion, and that had always worked well for both parties. On the other hand, Ewell had been conditioned by Jackson to expect and execute very specific orders. Second, Lee assumed he was sending his order to someone he knew well, but he failed to consider that everything he knew of his new corps commander came from observing Ewell as a *division* commander under Jackson.

Lieutenant General Richard Ewell (Library of Congress)

The action that day that brought Ewell to the foot of Cemetery Ridge was the first time Ewell was commanding an entire corps while under fire. Lee ought to have recognized he did not yet know what to expect from this "new" Ewell in the heat of combat, so he should have been very clear on his intent for Ewell at such a critical juncture in the battle. Instead, Lee framed his order just as he would have done for Jackson, anticipating it would produce the same kind of result. When it did not, Lee at least learned something important that night, something he should have known already—Ewell was *not* Jackson.

This speculation assumes that Lee intended his order to give Ewell the self-confidence to make his own decision, and if that is true, it worked. Ewell clearly did feel empowered to make a firm decision, but unfortunately for the Confederate Army, it was not the one Lee was anticipating. Lee was exhibiting good leadership by trying to tailor his task objective for the recipient, but it went wrong because Lee really didn't know his man as well as he needed to at that moment. There is an important leadership lesson here: when people change their places in the organization, much of what you thought you knew about them may have changed, too. It is time to start getting to know your people all over again . . .

ASSEMBLING A GREAT TEAM

In this chapter we have thoroughly explored the options great leaders can employ to develop team members who are ready to accept and execute well-defined tasks. However, before leaders ever have the opportunity to develop their people, someone has to assemble their team. It is therefore important to spend some time examining the question, "What can a leader do to assemble a great team in the first place?"

The answer will vary widely based on the leader's organization. Some leaders have considerable influence over the hiring and team construction process, while others have centralized functions in the organization to assemble and staff the teams. Each leader will have to navigate the specific norms of his own organization, but in every case, a great leader should be able to visualize the composition for his team that will enable mission accomplishment on a broad range of tasks.

It is self-evident that a team with a variety of capabilities will be able to accomplish more missions than a team suited to only perform the same kinds of tasks. Therefore, leaders who create teams whose members have diverse *skills* and *abilities* are generally creating stronger teams with a higher propensity to deliver wins than a team comprised of people who all have very similar backgrounds and experiences.

Lieutenant Colonel Scott Chambers, my civil engineers squadron commander at Bagram, once made a comment to me that illustrates the limitations from assembling a team whose members all come from the same mold. He said, "When the only tool in your box is a hammer, then the whole world looks like a nail." A good leader must prevent all his team members from being hammers or they will all apply the same type of solution to every problem. But if a leader can assemble a team with a wide range of skills and experience, her people will bring multiple perspectives to a thorny problem, and so can craft innovative solutions.

For instance, let's suppose a leader has a team with several members who are all highly skilled in detailed planning and record-keeping, but none of whom are comfortable coordinating activities with people from other teams. In essence, the entire team is built to process information, so the leader will have multiple options to win at tasks that need that specific skill. On the other hand, the leader currently has no one on the team who can manage stakeholders or collaborate effectively across the organization. That would obviously be a big hole in the team's skill set, especially if the organization requires a lot of cross-functional project work. Most forward-thinking leaders would conclude they'll be seeing tasks that require that skill set, so they'd better find a way to fill that hole.

The first option, of course, is to acquire the needed skill by developing it with one of the current team members. When this option is not feasible, then the leader will need to *import* that skill with a new hire to the team. There are several ways to do this, of course, and again, the organization's rules and resource limitations will probably dictate the options for the leader. But whether the new person comes from an internal swap with another team, an organizational change to add positions to the team, or just a timely vacancy due to normal turnover, the leader should still be guided by a single principle—hire for quality.

Quality as used here describes two different phases of the hiring process. In the traditional sense a "quality candidate" is one who exhibits superior performance in a certain space, so the leader needs to start by identifying only those candidates who will excel at the day-to-day work associated with the role and setting aside those who do not. Meanwhile, a "quality hire" is also someone who brings to the team additional skills and experiences the leader is specifically seeking. In the example above, that would be a candidate who is adept at working on projects with people from other teams.

Even when they don't have the final say on a hiring decision, most leaders can influence the job description being sent to candidates and thereby shape the candidate pool to match the needs of the moment and hopefully generate a list of high-quality applicants. Leaders should therefore be very proactive in crafting those job descriptions with unambiguous descriptions of the desired skills and experiences. If leaders have the opportunity to review the resumes or interview the candidates personally, they should probe the applicants' experiences and credentials in search of other critical skills that are in short supply on the team, especially those skills likely to be needed soon for upcoming tasks.

Every one of these hiring events offers an opportunity not only to fill an immediate gap, but to find people who can help the team accomplish more tasks over the long haul. If the leader does not go into the interview process with both an open mind and a clear sense of what the team's overall skills profile looks like at the moment, then she may well miss this opportunity to make the team stronger. The over-arching objective of assembling a team must be to maximize the team's chances of winning at every task.

I can think of a couple of examples where I was involved in this process, and both occurred as I was getting close to completing a command tour. Command positions at both the squadron and group level are filled with a three-step process. The first step is a screening: each officer who meets the eligibility criteria for rank and time in service may apply to a board that meets annually and determines which officers have the requisite leadership credentials to command at that level. The names of each officer that screened successfully are published on a public list and all command vacancies in the upcoming year must be filled by someone from that list. The second phase is bidding: all wing commanders review the list and submit a formal bid for the officers they would like to hire to fill the various vacancies in their wing, usually listing their top five choices for each position. The third step is assignment: the Personnel Center reviews and de-conflicts all the bids and attempts to optimize the final assignments so that each wing commander gets as many of the people they bid on as possible. There are of course numerous other inputs that can affect the final assignments, including development needs of specific officers and some inevitable politicking by senior generals and headquarters staffers, and this all goes into the mix, too.

As I was preparing to complete my squadron command tour at Charleston in 2006, my group commander asked me to look at the candidates from my career field who could take my place at the aerial port squadron. At the time, Charleston was the primary base for shipping cargo to our forces in Iraq and we were managing a lot of dynamic programs. As a result, we needed someone who knew the air transportation business inside and out and could jump into the command with both feet on Day One. Our focus was therefore on the initial phase of hiring for quality. I scored dozens of officers based on their reputations and their experiences and we were in the process of finalizing a bid list when a colonel from our headquarters called. He was the logistics officer career manager at the headquarters, and he told us he was already talking to the Personnel Center about who he wanted to see fill the few aerial port squadron commander vacancies coming up that year.

Our logistics career field had recently been created by merging the three previously separate career fields of transportation, supply, and logistics plans. As a result, we had a lot of officers my age who had worked almost exclusively in their original career field and thus did not have much experience in the other areas. The career field managers thus had a strong desire to broaden these officers any way they could. In this case, the colonel wanted to assign a former supply officer with no previous air transportation experience to run our aerial port as a broadening opportunity to fill that gap. While this officer would have brought a new expertise to the position, it was not expertise that was relevant to the job, so it really didn't make the group commander's team stronger (especially since he had another logistics squadron with plenty of supply expertise.)

More importantly, this officer did not fit the critical skills profile we determined was necessary to run this busy aerial port, and so we told the colonel we would not bid for that officer, even though he had a strong record. He simply didn't have the right core skills for this job, and so we would not have been hiring for quality. After a fair bit of back and forth debate with the career manager, we won out and actually got our first choice to take my place, while the officer we had passed on got his broadening at a smaller aerial port which was not much engaged in the war effort and thus was a great place for him to learn the trade.

A few years later, I found myself in a similar discussion about who should replace me as group commander at Bagram. In this case I was advising the wing commander directly and we had a host of candidates from several different career fields to consider. The screening board had largely addressed the first element of quality for us. Executive management of a large organization is the primary skill needed to command a group, and without that demonstrated skill, an officer would not have screened successfully, so we knew anyone on the list had already cleared that high entry bar.

We focused instead on the second element, which was to bring in broader experiences that would ensure the wing commander could accomplish all missions. In this case, we evaluated how to bring skills diversity to the group commander position at a more strategic level. Because my group consisted of six different squadrons with a wide array of missions, we wanted to ensure the group commander position was filled over time with people from different career fields to ensure no single mission had too much or too little oversight by senior leadership.

I had assumed command of the group the prior year from Colonel Patty Searcy, who was a personnel officer, while I brought logistics and air transportation experience to the position during my tenure. We therefore decided to look first for high-performing officers with backgrounds in civil engineering and security forces because these were two very important missions at Bagram at the time and it had been some years since the group commander had come from either of those backgrounds. We found several outstanding people on the list, and we placed our bids for those officers. One of those bids was a classmate of mine named Colonel Jeff Hunt, who was a career security forces officer, and it was to Jeff that I turned over command of the group a few months later.

Change of Command at Bagram 2010: Wing Commander Jack Briggs (left) prepares to transfer command of the 455th Expeditionary Mission Support Group from me (center) to Colonel Jeff Hunt (right)

In both of these cases, my bosses and I were very deliberate about the specific skills we did and did not need, and we invested heavily in researching each candidate to identify what they could bring to the team to make it stronger. This is what leaders at all levels should do every time they bring in a new member of their team. Making hiring and promotion decisions is really just another version of the process a successful leader uses to make the "right choice" when assigning a task, which is the subject of the next chapter. In that chapter we'll be discussing the principles for determining if a candidate will fail or can succeed, and those same principles work just as well when assembling a team. The only difference is that the leader choosing a new team member must evaluate which candidate will put *the whole team* in a better position to win. Those who do this well will have a big head start for building a deep bench.

CASE STUDY: HOW THE MESSIAH CAME TO KNOW HIS PEOPLE

"For whoever has will be given more, and they will have an abundance . . ."

J esus' earthly ministry lasted about three years. During that time he gained fame for his teachings about the Kingdom of Heaven and for the miracles he performed. However, a critical element of his program was to identify those who would carry his mantle after he was gone. Jesus therefore invested heavily in getting to know his people during this period.

As his fame grew, so did the number of disciples and followers who moved about with him and assisted in his mission of outreach. Jesus was in constant contact with these people—they ate together, traveled together, lodged together, and prayed and worshipped together. With such sustained contact, Jesus had ample opportunity to evaluate and understand his followers. He didn't stop with mere evaluation, but also invested heavily in training and encouraging growth. He had regular sessions with small groups, telling parables or training the participants in a deeper understanding of what God demanded of them. Jesus saw many grow in faith, spirit, understanding, and devotion as a result of these activities.

But Jesus also knew that the most profound growth in these areas comes from overcoming new challenges. He described an example of stretching subordinates to gauge their potential abilities in the *Parable of the Talents*. In this allegory, Jesus tells of a master who departs on a journey, but entrusts three of his servants with some of his money. He gives one servant five bags of gold, another servant two bags of gold and the third servant one bag of gold to see how they will handle the responsibility. In due time the master returns and calls the servants to account. The first two servants both doubled their master's money through shrewd investing. The master blesses each of these servants, saying "Well done, good and faithful servant! You have been faithful with a few things; I will put you in charge of many things. Come and share your master's happiness!" The third servant, however, followed a different strategy: "I was afraid and went out and hid your gold in the ground. See, here is what belongs to you." The master responded to his folly, "You wicked lazy servant . . . you should have [at least] put my money on deposit with the bankers, so that when I returned I would have received it back with interest. So take the bag of gold from him and give it to the one who has ten bags. For whoever has will be given more, and they will have an abundance. Whoever does not have, even what they have will be taken from them."[25]

Jesus' parable tells us he believed in stretching people to their full potential, but he also recognized people sometimes simply lack what it takes to do a job. He used this parable as a teaching point, but Jesus also practiced what he preached, actively stretching his followers to determine who had the potential to carry on for him after his crucifixion. Knowing there would be tribulations in the future for his adherents, he also told *The Parable of the Sower* to symbolize his followers' different levels of commitment to his cause:

> Listen! A farmer went out to sow his seed. As he was scattering the seed, some fell along the path, and the birds came and ate it up.

Some fell on rocky places, where it did not have much soil. It sprang up quickly, because the soil was shallow. But when the sun came up, the plants were scorched, and they withered because they had no root. Other seed fell among thorns, which grew up and choked the plants, so that they did not bear grain. Still other seed fell on good soil. It came up, grew and produced a crop, some multiplying thirty, some sixty, some a hundred times.[26]

Jesus later translated the analogies in this parable, explaining that it represented four different responses from those heard his Word:

1. Those who hear the Word and choose to ignore it.
2. Those who hear the Word and have a strong emotional reaction to it, but no depth of devotion, and so they fall away as soon as they face adversity.
3. Those who hear the Word and want to follow, but cannot escape the cares of daily living, so they too fall away.
4. Those who hear the Word and sincerely commit to it, fighting through challenges and distractions to "produce a crop."[27]

To accomplish his mission, the Messiah needed people who fell into that fourth category. Living with people on a daily basis gave him very valuable insights into the strengths, potential, and weaknesses of his closest followers, but he also looked for opportunities to put his leading candidates to the test. Jesus chose twelve specific followers to be his primary protégés.* The Bible reports that Jesus deliberately recruited most of this group, personally calling them to follow him. Although most of them were from Jesus' own home region of Galilee, they had very different personalities and strengths and brought an array of experiences. Perhaps seven of the twelve were fishermen, but two of them were likely also business owners who managed a workforce and one of them is believed to have been from a higher social standing due to his bloodlines. One was a tax collector who had worked for the Romans, two were political activists called *zealots*, and two others may have

---

* See *The Gospel of Mark* 3:13 for the full list of the original twelve apostles

been tradesmen of some kind. Judas Iscariot was assigned to manage the group's money-bag, so he likely had some experience in finance or administration. Jesus was clearly assembling a diverse team that would have members who could interact with all elements of the society.[28] He began to develop these outreach skills by sending the twelve out on a test mission, granting them great powers and challenges:

> Calling the Twelve to him, he began to send them out two by two and gave them authority over impure spirits. These were his instructions: "Take nothing for the journey except a staff—no bread, no bag, no money in your belts. Wear sandals but not an extra shirt. Whenever you enter a house, stay there until you leave that town. And if any place will not welcome you or listen to you, leave that place and shake the dust off your feet as a testimony against them." They went out and preached that people should repent.[29]

Apparently the twelve met the challenge, because the Bible confirms "they drove out many demons and anointed many sick people with oil and healed them."[30] Having stretched the men he would make his apostles, Jesus was not done. He sent out 72 more followers on a similar mission:

> [He] sent them two by two ahead of him to every town and place where he was about to go. He told them, "The harvest is plentiful, but the workers are few. Ask the Lord of the harvest, therefore, to send out workers into his harvest field. Go! I am sending you out like lambs among wolves." Jesus then went on to provide specific instructions about how they should travel, interact with the local population, and evaluate the houses and the towns where they stayed. He also gave them the power to heal the sick.[31]

Luke reports later that many came back increased in power and faith: "The seventy-two returned with joy and said, 'Lord, even the demons submit to us in your name!'"[32] The Gospels tell us no more details of the 72, but we can presume Jesus used the results to help identify additional strong leaders who might serve in other roles or be available to step up should more apostles be needed. As it turned out, a man name Matthias was selected to replace Judas Iscariot, after the latter betrayed Jesus and then committed suicide.[33] It is very possible Matthias was one of the 72 followers Jesus had sent out to prove themselves. Thanks to the long and focused effort he made to know and grow his people, Jesus built a deep bnch.

THE RIGHT CHOICE

Principle #4: Put Your People in a Position to Succeed

&

Principle #5: Don't Put Your People in a Position to Fail

T he sun was just going down when I arrived for duty as Officer-in-Charge (OIC) of the night shift during my first-ever Operational Readiness Inspection. In the six months since I had arrived at McChord Air Force Base as a brand-new second lieutenant in October of 1988, I had gone through a series of exercises leading up to the formal ORI that was upon us, so I was trained and ready to direct aerial port operations at Travis Air Force Base, which was serving as our "deployed airfield." I took a quick look at the duty roster and asked myself, "*What am I going to do with Sergeant Driver?*"

My day-to-day duty position within my squadron back at McChord was OIC of the Vehicle Management team. One of my people was Staff Sergeant "Driver," a junior sergeant who was struggling. Driver was already under scrutiny for some performance deficiencies when I joined the squadron, and so he did not have the full confidence of the unit's leadership. Because Driver knew this, he believed he was adding no value to the unit, and nothing depletes a service member's morale more than feeling like a non-contributor to the team's mission. As I got to know Sergeant Driver, I agreed with the consensus that he was not a top-tier NCO in terms of his leadership/supervisory skills—which were still developing—but I also recognized he did have the technical knowledge required to manage our vehicle operations duties.

Once we were in place at our deployed location during the ORI, I was determined to get the maximum value out of everyone on my shift, including Sergeant Driver. I thought about what I knew of Sergeant Driver and then I pulled him aside and told him, "I want you to be the vehicle control manager for this shift. You need to know where every assigned vehicle is at all times and make sure the aircraft loading teams working on the aircraft line never face a delay in their activities because they don't have the vehicles they need. I won't have time to look over your shoulder to double-check all this, so I am counting on you."

This wasn't just bluster—the team's success servicing the aircraft in a timely manner really did depend on having the right equipment available when needed, so Driver understood I was trusting him with an important task. He took this to heart and did an outstanding job. He maintained full accountability of all the vehicles, including tracking of any that were taken out of service for maintenance. He even had a moment of "heroism" when he diagnosed and replaced a blown fuse to get a stalled vehicle on the tarmac back into service. His performance that week was conveyed to the squadron leadership, and as a result he started to repair his reputation in the unit.

All of this was a real shot in the arm for Driver's morale. I also noticed that after that ORI, he held me in high personal esteem because I had believed in him and given him the chance to help the team succeed. While managing a handful of vehicles for a few days is a relatively small task in the grand scheme, for that NCO at that moment, it was the most important thing in the world, and he made sure he delivered. I recall thinking at the time "***This is what can happen when you put people in a position to succeed!***" That insight was the genesis for my understanding of the two critical principles covered in this chapter.

* * *

Once you have framed your task and built a deep bench, you have arrived at the moment for the most important decision. Making the right choice is the essence of the Leading to Win model, and it simply means determining which person is best suited for a given task and then assigning the task to that person. A leader who has effectively executed the prior two principles will be in a much better position to discern the right choice than one who has not because a good framing will reveal the skills required to accomplish the mission, while a leader with a deep bench will have access to a longer "short list" of suitable candidates for the task.

However, while these activities can better position the leader for success when making the right choice, they will not guarantee it. Ultimately this final decision requires its own rational analysis and an element of strategic thinking, particularly when there are multiple tasks and choices to be made at the same time. Principles #4 and #5 are the touchstones that will guide the decision process, and when applied properly, they can serve the leader as litmus tests for evaluating the candidates. The dual principles of this chapter may appear to be the same notion expressed by two different descriptions, but this is not the case. They instead resemble two sides of a coin—they are indisputably connected, yet simultaneously distinct in both meaning and application.

Dissecting Principles #4 and #5

The first of these two principles—put your people in a position to succeed—describes a leader taking positive actions to bring about *positive results*. The leader's goal here is to *intentionally align* a task's requirements with the team members' strengths to create the conditions where those strengths can be used to their fullest. Conversely, leaders apply the second principle—don't put your people in a position to fail—as a defense against *negative results*. In this case the leader's intent is to identify team members whose strengths do not match the task's "must have" requirements. A person with a strong positive alignment between task requirements and skills will be a strong candidate for the task, while a person with a misalignment between skills and task requirements should be excluded from the short list. The two principles typically work in tandem with one another, but before we explore the use of these companions together, let's first take each one in turn, using two of my own personal experiences to illustrate what makes each unique.

I cannot claim I assigned Sergeant Driver to his ORI task using a leadership model or a long, drawn-out analytical process. In reality the analysis happened in a matter of seconds, and it was only later that I reflected upon what I had done in that instant and how it fit into a larger model of leadership. Although everything happened pretty organically, what transpired was nonetheless exactly how a leader intentionally Leading to Win would have made the right choice in that situation.

Principle #4 requires a leader to look at a task's requirements and the team members' skill sets and then ask, "Where do I see opportunities?" When our shift assembled, I looked at all the team members and matched them to the tasks they needed to perform. Most were pre-assigned before the deployment began, but I had latitude to use Sergeant Driver for whatever purpose I wanted, and what I wanted was to give him a real task that would help us excel on the ORI. I knew Driver well by that time (Principle #2) and I was confident he had the accountability skills and a sufficient understanding of our fleet's operational demands to prevent us from running short on vehicles for the aircraft loading teams. Since those were exactly the skills the vehicle controller task called for, I had a positive alignment (Principle #4) and I assigned him the task. Note that I then framed the task for Sergeant Driver (Principle #1) by defining a clear *objective* for him, including the context about why the task mattered. Putting his name on the roster as the Vehicle Controller also granted him the *authorities* he needed to direct the use of each vehicle. In the end Sergeant Driver delivered a win on the vehicle control task, and because that task ensured the availability of critical *resources* for our team's larger mission of loading and unloading aircraft in a safe and timely manner, we delivered a win on that mission, too. In fact our operations contributed to the Wing's overall ORI grade of OUTSTANDING, the highest score possible and one rarely given.

Ten years later, though, I found myself applying Principle #5, and the story didn't have such a happy ending. That was the day I acknowledged that even good leaders have to recognize when they can't win at a task. In Chapter 3, I described my framing for a project to build an On-the-Job Training (OJT) syllabus for my Airmen at Charleston. I indicated it was a big success, but it was also a long-time coming because that was not the first time I attempted the project. I originally discerned the need for a better training process and conceived of the syllabus idea while commanding the transportation squadron at Scott Air Force Base five years earlier. At Charleston, my training manager was a senior NCO and he grasped the advantages of the syllabus immediately, so he was energized to make the program work. Likewise, my senior technical experts also saw the benefits and were equally eager to assemble the syllabus. I put all these people in a position to succeed, and they did. However, I faced a completely different set of circumstances during my first attempt.

My training manager at Scott was quite junior and she simply could not understand what I was proposing. From her perspective, she had explained to me several times how the OJT program worked, and so she could not figure out why I kept babbling on about this "syllabus" thing, which was NOT part of the program. The subject matter experts to whom I floated this were only slightly less baffled when I asked them if they could align the tasks in a more logical manner; their response to the idea was to show me that all the tasks were already listed in the training folder and the training standards were already written. No one I spoke with seemed to understand I wanted them to transcend the existing program because of its shortcomings.

Then a major, I assumed command of the 375th Transportation Squadron at Scott Air Force Base in 1999. I developed the OJT Syllabus concept at Scott, but I could not implement it there.

After several weeks of trying to get traction on the concept, I concluded this was an idea whose time had not yet come—at least not in this unit—and so I put it on the shelf for another day. I had decided not to pursue the project further because I would have been putting my people in a position to fail. Had I tried to push this initiative with the people I had to execute it, the only result would have been mutual frustration from all parties because I would have been asking them to do something they clearly didn't understand and would likely not have been able to deliver. This was not a case where a better framing of the task would have resolved the confusion, nor was it an opportunity to "stretch" the training manager. It was simply a situation where the task was beyond the reach of my team.

I chose these two personal examples to emphasize the different attributes of each principle, and while I think the stories serve that purpose well, I also recognize they are somewhat simplistic. That is, I obviously gave Sergeant Driver a task where he could succeed rather than a task on which he was likely to fail. Similarly, I chose not to pursue the OJT task at Scott because the only people available to do it would probably have failed. I would expect anyone else to reach the same conclusions in the same situations even if they never read this book. However, real-world situations are often more complex, and leaders won't apply these principles effectively unless they have developed through practice the specific mindset that enables them to assess the circumstances and consistently make the ideal people-to-task assignments to accomplish their mission.

PUTTING ALL THE PRINCIPLES TOGETHER

A great leader must become adept at thinking more conceptually about these principles and especially their interplay with each other. The two principles need to act as handrails that can channel a leader to optimal task assignment decisions in complex circumstances. In more weighty situations than the personal cases I described, outcomes will be much more dynamic and significant. There may be multiple decisions in play, some of which will drive success or failure for another task. The leader's challenge and opportunity is to orchestrate the outcomes so as to maximize the degree of mission accomplishment possible.

Stephen Ambrose's excellent book *Band of Brothers* chronicles a story from World War II that illustrates the virtuoso use of this technique. The action takes place within the 506th Parachute Infantry Regiment under the command of Colonel Robert Sink. The Easy Company commander was Captain Herbert Sobel, and during the regiment's training period, Sobel pushed his men very hard. As a result Easy Company became one of the best-conditioned and most technically skilled units in the regiment. However, Captain Sobel was not beloved by his troops—officer or enlisted. He was particularly abusive toward Lieutenant Dick Winters, perhaps because the enlisted troops respected Winters' natural leadership abilities and so they were quick to follow him. Meanwhile, they were very reluctant to follow Captain Sobel because his training skills were much more effective than his field skills. Many of the NCOs were afraid Sobel would literally get them all killed in a real combat situation. Sobel eventually made life so difficult for Winters that the latter was moved out of Easy Company, and with D-Day imminent, the unit's NCOs were desperate. Ambrose takes up the story from there:

> With Winters gone, Sobel still in charge, and combat coming, the N.C.O.s were in an uproar. Sergeants Ramsay and Harris called a meeting. Ramsey and Harris proposed that they present Colonel Sink with an ultimatum: either Sobel be replaced or they would turn in their stripes.
>
> This radical proposal elicited much comment, many questions, great concern, but in the end the group decision was that going into combat under Sobel's command was unthinkable. The only way they could let [battalion commander Lieutenant Colonel Robert] Strayer and Sink know how strongly they felt was to turn in their stripes. Each noncom thereupon wrote out his own resignation. . . . The N.C.O.s then thought further about what they were doing and decided to consult with Winters. He was invited to the orderly room, where on arrival Ramsey told him what the group had done.
>
> "Don't," said Winters. "Don't even think about it. This is mutiny." . . .
>
> By this time the whole battalion was talking about Sobel's battles, first with Winters and now with his N.C.O.s. Sink would have had to have been deaf, dumb and blind not to have been aware. He should also have been grateful that Winters had talked the N.C.O.s out of presenting him with an ultimatum. A few days later, Sink came down to Company E, called all the noncoms together, and as

[Sergeant] Lipton recalled, "Gave us hell. He told us we disgraced our company and that he could put every one of us in the guardhouse for years. As we were preparing for combat, he said that it could be called mutiny in the face of the enemy for which we could be shot."

Fortunately for Sink, the 101st Airborne had just established a Parachute Jumping school at the nearby village of Chilton Foliat, in order to qualify as paratroopers doctors, chaplains, communications men, forward artillery observers, and others who would be jumping on D-Day. Who better than Sobel to run a training camp?

Sink sent Sobel to Chilton Foliat and . . . he made 1st Lt Thomas Meehan of Baker [Company] the C.O. [Commanding Officer] of Easy. And he brought Winters back, as leader of the 1st platoon. Sergeant Ramsay was busted to private and Harris was transferred. The Sobel era of Easy Company had come to an end.

Meehan was Sobel's opposite. Slender, fairly tall, willowy, he had common sense and competence. He was strict but fair, he had good voice command. "Under Meehan," Winters said, "we became a normal company."[34]

Let's critique Colonel Sink's performance here using the two principles in this chapter as the measuring rods and—spoiler alert! – he scores an A+ . . .

Colonel Sink's priority was his objective. His regiment was going to be among the first units to hit the ground on D-Day and his mission task was to secure the flanks of the landing beaches and disrupt the German rear until the invading forces could make their way inland. The paratroopers would be largely operating out on a limb and if they were to succeed, every company had to be well-led.

Emblem of Colonel Robert Sink's 506th Parachute Infantry Regiment (U.S. Army Institute of Heraldry)

Colonel Sink also knew his people. He knew Sobel had been the best training officer in the regiment, so this was clearly a real strength of Sobel's. However, Sink was now discovering that Sobel's combat command skills and his ability to inspire his troops were clearly weaknesses. He also knew the leadership qualities of several other junior officers in the regiment. Finally, he knew the NCOs of Easy Company well enough to be sure they were all professionals ready to fight, so their mutiny stunt had to be driven by a sincere lack of confidence in Sobel's leadership.

So, what to do about it all?

Colonel Sink first addressed the mutiny. Even though he understood what motivated the action, he couldn't allow it to stand. He made examples of the ring-leaders, but did not decimate the whole team of NCOs. His removal of Sergeants Ramsay and Harris ensured he didn't put Easy Company in a position to fail. Had those two been left in place, the other NCOs may have shifted their allegiance from the commanding officers to those two NCOs, which in the long run would have destroyed unit cohesion in combat. By the same token, his decision to forgive the rest of the NCOs put Easy Company in a position to succeed in battle because those NCOs were critical front-line leaders whose skills would be crucial in combat actions.

Next up were the officers. Sending Easy Company into the field under Sobel's command was clearly not an option. Sobel's lack of field leadership skill was an irredeemable weakness, so Sink would have been putting Sobel in a position to fail if he left the captain in place. The cost of that failure may have been the loss of every soldier in Easy Company, not to mention the negative impact on the D-Day mission itself. On the other hand, Sobel did have proven skills training paratroopers for their mission, and as luck would have it, there was a need for an experienced trainer elsewhere at that same moment.

While it may have been humiliating for Sobel when Sink reassigned him from Easy Company to Chilton Foliat, Sink was actually putting Sobel in a position to succeed, and moreover, to help the Airborne Division succeed because the support forces going though Sobel's school would be well-prepared for combat, too. Finally, with Sobel out of the regiment, Sink was able to tap some lieutenants who had proven leadership skills and put them, and by extension all of Easy Company, into a position to succeed.

Faced with a really ugly set of circumstances, Colonel Sink employed all the right principles, moving his pieces around the board until everyone was in the best place to *win*. The battlefield accomplishments of Easy Company as related in the rest of Ambrose's book are testimony that Sink was Leading to Win.

THE TWO CRITICAL QUESTIONS FOR MAKING THE RIGHT CHOICE

Every leader in any organization can be as effective as Colonel Sink was. As I pointed out at the beginning of the chapter, before doing anything else, a leader needs to review the task objective, enumerate the skills required to complete the task, and then review the strengths/weaknesses profile of the team members. Sometimes making the right choice is nearly automatic because the skills match—or mismatch—is so obvious. When it isn't so clear or when there are multiple possibilities, then the leader may have to depend on instinct and judgment to make the call, and in these cases Principles #4 and #5 can be a good sanity check. To use them to full effect, the leader must first evaluate each of his candidates' qualities carefully and then ask himself two questions.

First, he needs to apply Principle #5 and ask himself, "Will I be putting this candidate in a position to fail?" Unless the answer is an emphatic "NO," then the candidate *cannot* be the right choice. Any expressions of uncertainty here—"probably not" or "I don't *think* so"—are disqualifiers. By putting all the candidates through this narrow gate, the leader will winnow the field quickly. It is an objective test that helps a leader set aside emotions and de-personalize the decision.

I very nearly failed this test myself, and I am a little embarrassed to say it happened at a point in my career where I ought to have been old enough to know better. While commanding my group in Afghanistan, we had to medically evacuate my logistics squadron commander. He had developed a severe back condition that was putting him at serious risk of an injury that could have crippled him. He wanted more than anything to tough it out through the end of this tour, and as much as I admired his fortitude, I wouldn't let him take that risk just to satisfy pride, so we ordered him home for surgery. That suddenly left me without a commander for a squadron that needed a strong leader.

The normal procedure for getting a replacement commander in a situation like this was to alert the Air Force that we needed an emergency backfill, and our personnel center would send us an officer who had formally screened for squadron command. More often than not, this would be someone who was already in command at a stateside base, which could have left a leadership gap in that unit. To prevent that from happening, I came up with a different idea. I wanted us to look around the combat theater and find someone who was already deployed and bring them to Bagram. I hit upon the idea because we had heard of a qualified officer whose original tasking was ending, but as it turned out that person was already reassigned and was not available. I then started looking around for *any* logistics officer of the right rank. I found someone and got it in my head this was an ideal solution.

Why was I so determined to find someone locally? Well, one practical reason was that I thought we'd get someone quicker, but I also had a blind spot from a previous personal experience. I had been deployed to Iraq on short notice from my aerial port squadron four years earlier. Professionally, the deployment was a good thing for me, but I always felt that taking me away from the unit at Charleston was bad for our squadron because we were shipping the lion's share of critical air cargo to the combat zone. I was trying to prevent another squadron from suddenly losing its commander, but I was concentrating on the wrong objective. My task in Afghanistan was to provide outstanding logistics support to the warfighters at my own base, and I should have been completely focused on making the right choice for a leader I needed to manage that task. Instead, I was worried about how to maintain stability at some other squadron at a U.S. base. That base had its own group commander, and it was that leader's task to manage any leadership shortfalls within that squadron.

More to the point, I was not even applying the very test I described for this principle because the candidate I found was far from ideal anyway. One of the staff officers at our wing knew him by reputation and that reputation was not great. I then called his current supervisor in Afghanistan and asked, "Is this guy up to commanding a squadron?" His answer was, "Let me tell you about him. I promise, he will . . . WORK . . . for . . . you!" This was emphatic, but not really a ringing endorsement for command, either, but since it wasn't an outright rejection I thought *maybe, possibly* he wouldn't fail, and *hopefully* the responsibility wouldn't be beyond him. From a starting imperative to bring in a strong leader, I had somehow drifted to a place where I was rationalizing that I could make do with an officer of dubious quality.

As a lieutenant colonel in 2006, I was deployed to Baghdad, Iraq, on short notice to serve as the advisor to the Director of Logistics of the re-forming Iraqi Air Force. The deployment was an important career event for me, but it took me away from command of my squadron at Charleston Air Force Base.

Fortunately, my own commander intervened and directed me to follow the normal route and request a fully qualified officer from wherever the Air Force decided to send one. Once he had pulled me back from the cliff I was about to walk over, I recovered my perspective and saw where I had gone off the rails in my thinking. It all ended really well because we got Lieutenant Colonel Travis Condon, who in the few short months he was with us completed the revitalization of the logistics squadron. But it could have been a disaster because I was willing to keep an open mind when the answer to the question, "Am I setting him up to fail?" was clearly not a hard "NO!" So learn from my near miss, and *don't ever* compromise on this point.

Once the leader has *correctly* applied Principle #5 to define a short list, she then must ask herself the critical Principle #4 question: "Will I be putting my candidate in a position to succeed?" In this case the answers do not need to be absolute, and in fact, conditional answers may help with the decision. In all likelihood, the answer is going to lean toward some version of "yes" or the candidates wouldn't be on the short list in the first place, but in this case the responses can be nuanced, and the various descriptors can be ranked. For instance, the answer "I'm pretty confident" beats "maybe" which beats "only if everything goes right with the plan." Principle #4 thus becomes a sorting tool to stratify the candidates' opportunities to succeed. The leader can then quickly separate the truly best candidate from a pack of viable options.

On occasion, a leader will have a short list of folks who all earn an "Absolutely" when this question is posed, which is always a nice problem to have. In these cases the *best* choice isn't always the right choice. There are a number of reasons why a leader might assign a task to someone who was not at the very top of the list, and they generally support an optimization strategy for the broader team. For instance,

- A leader may choose not to use Candidate A because that person is consistently the top choice for tough assignments, and the leader needs to "spread the wealth" to avoid burning out Candidate A or making Candidate A an object of resentment for everyone else waiting for their chance to contribute
- A leader may choose Candidate B over Candidate A simply because Candidate B needs the recognition a win will garner, and this task is a perfect means to that end
- A leader who has a series of tasks to assign may choose Candidate C in order to employ Candidates A and B on other tasks. One candidate cannot do all the tasks at once even if the person is the best candidate for all of them, so the leader finds the best line-up that will deliver wins on every task

Such combinations and rationales are endless, and they can enhance the team's overall mission accomplishment rate, but a combination is only optimal when every assigned task adheres to Principle #4 and doesn't violate Principle #5. Great leaders have a knack for making this calculus work repeatedly.

DEDICATION: A PREREQUISITE FOR EVERY TASK ASSIGNMENT

There is, however, one other caveat the leader needs to remember as he assesses his people against Principle #4, and it is this: putting a person in a position to succeed does not *guarantee* success. Mission accomplishment also requires the tasked person to accept the challenge and fully employ their abilities. Here is where Principle #2 comes back into play. (Isn't it neat how all the principles support one another?) A leader who genuinely knows her people should also know when someone will not show enough dedication to a given task to be trusted with responsibility for the task. A leader who chooses someone without the motivation to win on a task—even when that someone has an otherwise ideal skill set for the task – is ultimately putting that person in a position to fail. Therefore, personal dedication to the mission must always be considered a necessary strength for any task.

I learned this lesson the hard way early in my career. I mentioned in Chapter 1 that I had the privilege of being the commander of my cadet squadron during the fall semester of my senior year at the Air Force Academy. With the position came the authority to appoint my classmates to the various staff positions within the squadron. Since I had been living and working with all of these people in very close quarters for the previous two years, I knew them all very well. I also knew what traits made for a successful candidate in each of the staff roles. I was thus able to build what I thought would be an effective leadership team because I was literally putting people in positions where I expected them to succeed. For the most part it worked well, but I did fall short in one area.

Each cadet squadron has a program that is essentially a Quality Assurance function designed to ensure all aspects of the unit's activities are meeting established standards. Our unit had not scored well in this area the previous couple of years and I wanted to change that. My objective was to ace the standards inspection we would face. I needed three people who paid attention to detail, focused on quality, possessed a continuous improvement mindset, and had the leadership skills to correct sub-par performance. As it happened, I thought I had three perfect candidates for this job. They all had the strengths that would make them ideal for the task and I was sure they would get us where we needed to be. I was also influenced by what I saw as an additional personal benefit for each of them.

The staff positions each come with a cadet officer rank and the higher rank signifies higher prestige, but only for that one semester.

As a Cadet First Class in Fall 1987, I commanded Cadet Squadron 2. Among my duties were assigning my classmates to their staff positions and leading the unit on parade.

In the spring, all the jobs including the commander are reshuffled. Generally, those with lower ranks in the fall get more senior positions in the spring and vice-versa. Nonetheless, everyone seems to lobby for their dream job in the fall semester. Of course, for every cadet who lands a choice role, several others are disappointed.

All three of my choices were hoping for a "big" job, but I could not accommodate them because I had other candidates I preferred for those roles. I did, however, believe they were worthy of the top-level jobs they were seeking, so I wanted to set them up to be the leading candidates for those positions in the spring. Because of the way the end-of-semester shuffle typically worked, I honestly believed I was helping them most by assigning them to less prestigious roles so they'd be well-positioned to compete for the jobs they really wanted in the next semester. More importantly, I knew that if they did earn accolades by turning around our standards program, they would also have even stronger resumes for the top roles they wanted in the spring. From my perspective, this was going to be a strategic win for everyone.

Unfortunately, none of the three people I tapped for these roles saw it through my lens. Instead, they felt they had been cheated and disrespected, and when I explained why I wanted strong players in that role and how I expected it to give them the inside track for something even better in the spring, they remained unconvinced. The result was that all three of them chose to put no significant effort into the task that semester and so my vision of a top-notch standards program never materialized. It was a personal disappointment, but also an important leadership lesson that I never forgot—ability alone won't deliver wins.

Interesting war stories aside, some of this discussion may seem a bit academic. Surely the benefits of putting someone in a position to succeed and the detriments of putting someone in a position to fail are readily apparent to even mediocre leaders. And how many *great* leaders really sit down and go through such a regimented exercise whenever they need to assign someone to an important task? In truth, most great leaders who consistently make the right choice do so because it has become their natural way of thinking, but it is unlikely they were simply born with this capacity.

These leaders almost certainly developed their skill over time from practical experience and probably some mistakes that made an impression, just like my own. My point in presenting such a deliberate procedure for making the right choice is to help leaders internalize the process. To that end, I have included Appendix 2 at the end of the book, which is a worksheet that any leader can use to help build the self-discipline to follow this methodology. Whether leaders sit down with a pen and formally fill out the form or just use it as a visual cue card for executing each step of the model, walking through this routine just a few times will be enough to train their minds to subconsciously adopt this logic whenever they have a task to assign. That's Leading to Win!

THE POWER OF RECOGNITION

However, once the task is complete, once the mission is accomplished and you have notched the win, you still have one last duty. You must celebrate the win. Sometimes that literally means throwing a party, but before you pop the champagne or cut the cake, you need to tell the world it was a win and who was behind it. (Hint – *that's not you!*) If you are Leading to Win, you won't need to highlight your own role in the process because your reputation will build itself as people see how many wins your team racks up.

Instead, the leader's role here is to make a big deal about the outcome and give credit to the person or people who delivered on the task, because everyone deserves recognition when they have done something special. Honest acclaim is priceless to most people, no matter where they are in life or in the organization. Here is a wonderful story of public praise told by Lieutenant General George C. Kenney, who was Douglas MacArthur's air commander in the Southwest Pacific during World War II. MacArthur was infamous for his own thirst for public adoration, but apparently, he knew how to give it, too:

> I got quite a kick that day out of a report of a MacArthur press conference. Some of the newspaper crowd told me about it. The General had finished his talk, when one of the correspondents said, "General, what is the Air Force doing today?" General MacArthur said, "Oh, I don't know. Go ask General Kenney." The newspaperman said, "General, do you mean to say you don't know where the bombs are falling?" MacArthur turned to him, grinned, and said, "Of course I know where the bombs are falling. They are falling in the right place. Go ask General Kenney where that is."

That was the best compliment I've ever received.[35]

If even a three-star general needs to feel the love sometimes, imagine what a few kind words can do for a young man or woman trying to build their own confidence!

As important as the recognition is for a person's self-image, your real strategic target for this publicity is the leadership *above* you. Every task your subordinates conquer is also a developmental step. They gain experience and competence and become ever more ready to move up a level and manage

General MacArthur personally decorating Lieutenant General George Kenney for the Air Force's actions during the Battle of the Bismarck Sea
(Australia @ War Collection)

teams of their own. It is your job as the leader to broadcast their achievements to the people who can promote them into those positions. Leaders who fight for their people inspire their people. Inspired people admire their leaders and yearn to emulate them. Great leadership begets great leadership. Your protégés will aspire to lead their people as effectively as you led them, and even if they don't know it, they'll soon be Leading to Win, too.

This certainly happened to me. My mentor Colonel Monti assigned me a series of high-visibility tasks while I was working for him, and every time I delivered, he made sure his bosses knew about it. He fought so hard for me that our general ranked me as the #1 captain in the Logistics Directorate during my final year there, and that led directly to a promotion to major two years earlier than normal. Colonel Monti absolutely made it a priority to develop me for future leadership roles. You can bet I admired him for it, and I strove to exhibit as many of his great leadership qualities as I could in the years that followed. And of course, one of the most important traits I emulated was the concept of finding success by matching the right people to the right tasks. In the assignments that followed, I had numerous opportunities to formulate and practice the Leading to Win concepts, particularly during two squadron commands, a group command in a war zone, and as the leader of a multi-service staff directorate. No matter what the task or setting, this model served me very well, and I hope it will help you win, too!

Now both retired from the Air Force, Colonel Virgil Monti and I are reunited at Randolph Air Force Base in 2023 in front of the Logistics Directorate building where we worked together from 1995-1997

CASE STUDY: THE MESSIAH MAKES THE RIGHT CHOICE

At once he left their nets and followed him . . .

There were two main phases to Jesus' human activities. The first phase was Jesus' ministry itself, wherein he shared all he knew about the Kingdom of God with the people of his own generation living in and around the province of Judea. All the signs he performed and the messages he proclaimed during this ministry laid the doctrinal foundation for his visionary second phase, which was to establish a community to share his Good News with all succeeding generations after his ascension. This second phase would have to be implemented by his followers after he was gone, so Jesus' most pressing need before he faced the cross was to designate the leaders who could make his vision a reality.

In a previous chapter of this case study, we looked at the task Jesus was framing and found that his objective was to create a common body of believers—the Church—and then extend its reach "to the ends of the earth." In the next chapter, we reviewed examples of how Jesus came to know and develop his closest followers. It is now time to see how Jesus applied the principles in this chapter to make the right choice for *the* leader of his Church.

Jesus was looking for two important attributes when evaluating a follower's readiness to lead the Church. He first needed people with real **commitment** and he set that bar very high, as this lesson from the *Gospel of Luke* demonstrates:

As they were walking along the road, a man said to him, "I will follow you wherever you go." Jesus replied, "Foxes have dens, and birds have nests, but the Son of Man has no place to lay his head." He said to another one, "Follow me." But he replied, "Lord, first let me go and bury my father." Jesus said to him, "Let the dead to bury their own dead, but you go and proclaim the kingdom of God." Still another said, "I will follow you Lord; but first let me go back and say goodbye to my family." Jesus replied, "No one who puts a hand to the plow and looks back is fit for service in the kingdom of God."[36]

These passages show that Jesus wanted potential followers to be clear they were asking to live a lifestyle that would be austere and demanding. His purpose in rejecting these followers could appear heartless when taken out of context, but that was not his intent. Instead, he wanted everyone to understand the full cost of following him. If someone wanted to be among those who picked up his mantle to carry out his legacy, then they had best be prepared to put that mission above *everything* else, including their family ties. With apologies to the Blues Brothers, these people truly would be on a "mission from God," and nothing else could take precedence.

As Jesus explained in the *Parable of the Sower* (see Chapter 4 case study), followers driven primarily by emotional zeal would soon fall away, and so Jesus had to identify and reject those people up front. Here is another occasion where he made certain he was not putting someone in a position to fail:

As Jesus started on his way, a man ran up to him and fell on his knees before him. "Good teacher, what must I do to inherit eternal life?" . . .

Jesus answered . . . "You know the commandments: You shall not murder, you shall not commit adultery, you shall not steal, you shall not bear false testimony, you shall not defraud, honor your father and mother."

"Teacher," he declared, "all these I have kept since I was a boy." Jesus looked at him and loved him. "One thing you lack," he said, "Go sell everything you have and give to the poor, and you will have treasure in heaven. Then come, follow me." Disheartened by the saying, he went away sorrowful for he had great possessions.[37]

Jesus probably did not doubt the young man's *sincerity* in wanting to follow him, but he did doubt the required level of commitment. He offered the young man a test of that commitment, and it proved to be a test the young man could not pass. Jesus' purpose was not malicious; on the contrary, the story emphasized that Jesus looked at the man and "loved" him. Jesus simply knew that if he took this young man as a disciple, he would be putting the young man in a position to fail, which would not have advanced Jesus' agenda or helped the young man's faith in the long run.

And speaking of **faith**, that is the second attribute Jesus was looking for in his prospective leader because the task would not be a pleasant one. The designated leader's message of love and salvation would often be met with hatred and disparagement. The leader of the Church would have to find a way to build congregations of followers in hostile communities who sought to drive him away, or worse. He would face constant abuse and even outright persecution, all with no worldly recompense or personal benefits. Only someone who believed absolutely in who Jesus was and what Jesus taught could successfully build the Church under these conditions. The Church's leader had to possess an unshakeable faith in the righteousness of the mission.

Jesus had narrowed his candidates down to the twelve named disciples who had the requisite commitment, and he envisioned important apostolic missions for all of them. But he still needed to choose one to stand above the rest as head of the Church. If Jesus was going to put someone in a position to succeed at launching and sustaining the Church, that person had to have real faith. Perhaps this is why there are so many verses in the Gospels where Jesus challenges, chastises, and encourages the disciples about their insufficiency of faith. We can also sense Jesus' frustration at times because even though he knew the disciples were all sincere in their desire to carry out his plans (well, at least 11 were), they nonetheless consistently failed to "get it."

On one occasion, several disciples even got into an argument about who would be considered the "greatest" once Jesus was gone, while in another passage, the mother of two of the disciples petitioned Jesus to assign her sons to the most prominent positions on his right and left side in heaven.[38] There is even a story of one disciple, Thomas, who refused to believe Jesus had been resurrected unless "I see the nail marks in his hands and put my finger where the nails were, and put my hand into his side."[39] The resurrected Jesus later gave Thomas this opportunity, and then commented in what one imagines was a slightly wry tone, "Blessed are those who have *not* seen and yet have believed."[40]

Jesus was no doubt exasperated as the disciples continued to focus on worldly honors rather than demonstrate true faith. Indeed, right until the end several disciples were still not clear about who Jesus truly was, even though he had told them over and over. However, there was one disciple who consistently redeemed his many human flaws with his faith:

- When Jesus called to him on his fishing boat, "at once [he] left their nets and followed him."[41]
- When he saw Jesus walking on the water, he immediately called out "'Lord if it's you . . . tell me to come to you on the water.'" 'Come' he said. . . . [and he] got down out of the boat, walked on the water and came toward Jesus"[42] until his fear overtook him and he began to flounder.
- When he initially refused Jesus' offer to wash his feet and Jesus rebuked him saying, "Unless I wash you, you have no part with me," he responded by saying "Lord, not just my feet but my hands and my head as well!"[43]

This disciple was named Simon and even though he, too, would fail a faith test when Jesus was taken away to be crucified, Jesus saw within him the authentic faith he sought, especially after Simon's spontaneous declaration that Jesus was the Messiah:

> When Jesus came to the region of Caesarea Philippi, he asked his disciples, "Who do people say the Son of Man is?"
>
> And they said, "Some say John the Baptist; others say Elijah; and still others Jeremiah or one of the prophets."
>
> "But what about you?" he asked. "Who do *you* say I am?"
>
> Simon Peter answered, "***You are the Messiah, the Son of the living God***."
>
> Jesus replied, "Blessed are you, Simon son of Jonah, for this was not revealed to you by flesh and blood, but by my father in heaven. And I tell you, you are Peter ["the rock"], and on this rock I will build my church, and the gates of Hades will not overcome it. I will give you the keys to the kingdom of heaven; whatever you bind on earth will be bound in heaven and whatever you loose on earth will be loosed in heaven." [44]

This "Great Confession" convinced Jesus that Peter had the faith required to accomplish the mission of building the Church. Appointing Peter to head the Church and as *de facto* leader of the apostles put all of them in a position to succeed. And succeed they did: all the apostles except Judas Iscariot traveled to the ends of the earth—from England to India, according to Church lore—proclaiming the Good News of salvation through Jesus Christ and converting thousands. All but St. John died martyr's deaths in the process, so their commitment and faith proved to be absolute. Peter himself was crucified in Rome and is buried beneath the altar of St. Peter's Basilica, the symbolic throne of Peter's successors for nearly 20 centuries.* Today, nearly one-third of the world's population—including

---

* Technically there was a previous St. Peter's basilica that stood from the 4th to the 16th centuries, so there have been two structures, but on the same location, and

people from every nation on the globe—claims a Christian faith, while the total number of souls pledged to Jesus since his time on Earth is too numerous to estimate. Peter truly was the Right Choice!

---

both home to the papal throne, which has been passed down in an unbroken line from Peter to the present day.

The *Leading To Win* Quick Reference Guide

This chapter is simply a recap of the main points presented throughout the book. It is meant to be a handy quick reference guide for reviewing the key themes, principles, and recommended activities encompassed within the Leading to Win model. It is not, however, an outline of the entire book, so the detailed descriptions, personal stories, historical examples, and case studies associated with each topic are not included in this chapter. Readers who want to re-examine the full treatment of any point made in the outline should refer back to the chapter where that point is discussed.

* * *

Chapter 1: Introducing *Leading To Win*

I. ***If you want a task done right, then assign the right person to do it!***
   A. This is the essence of leadership.
   B. This is the inspiration for the Leading to Win model.

II. Assigning the right person for a task sounds simple enough, but it doesn't happen naturally. Great leaders have learned how to do this instinctively.

III. The most effective leaders develop analytical habits that allow them to apply this leadership skill consistently.

IV. Leading to Win is a simple but effective leadership model with a set of principles that helps leaders master this skill set.

Chapter 2: What is Great Leadership?

I. Assessing great leadership is difficult because it is a highly subjective endeavor, so *Leading to Win* purposely uses intentionally narrow definitions that are more objective.

II. ***Successful leadership is the ability to consistently lead teams to do important tasks right;*** it is the ability to successfully "accomplish the mission."
    A. "Great" leaders are those leaders who do this repeatedly and commonly exhibit certain traits as a result.
        1. They are the leaders who always bring out the most from every member of their teams.
        2. They are the leaders whose teams can seemingly solve any problem.
        3. They are the leaders with the reputation for constantly delivering what the organization needs.

    B. The goal of *Leading to Win* is to help build such leaders.
    C. Great Leaders generally possess additional positive attributes that complement Leading to Win concepts, but which are not examined within the model itself, including:
        1. Having a reliable moral compasses.
        2. Showing genuine respect and concern for their people.
        3. Providing selfless service to the organization's success.

    D. ***A leader's main priority/purpose must be accomplishing today's mission,*** but developing future leaders is also an important aspect of leadership.
        1. Development must never be mistaken as the main priority.
        2. Development can often be accomplished in conjunction with the main priority.

E. A **task** in this context is defined as the job to be done.
  1. An important task is one whose successful outcome matters to the organization.
  2. Task complexity can vary widely and does not by itself define a task's importance.
  3. The right outcome or end state is defined by the leader who envisioned the task.

F. The process of delivering a successful result, or producing the right outcome, or achieving the desired end state is called **winning.**
G. Leading to Win principles are universal.
  1. These principles can be used by any leader at any level of any organization that has important tasks.
  2. The principles can also be applied to any task, irrespective of its nature or scope.

Chapter 3: The Task

Principle #1 Frame it Up

I. ***Effective leaders employ complete and coherent framings for their tasks in order to ensure their teams fully understand all elements of the task and successfully accomplish the mission.***

II. Each leader should develop a Framing methodology that works best for their style.
  A. The Leading to Win model recommends using written framing documents to ensure clarity of intent and prevent loss of important detail.
  B. Framing documents should not be too long; a limit of 2-3 pages is recommended.
III. A framing methodology should encompass at least the following four key elements in some form or fashion.

A. The **Objective**
1. Describes WHAT must be done, including the required end state.
2. When additional context is required to explain the WHY behind the task, it should be included in the objective section.
3. The length of the objective description may vary from a few words to multiple paragraphs.
4. The objective may include **sub-tasks.**
   a. Sub-tasks identify distinct aspects of the task, help refine the right outcome for the task, and can serve to outline a more complex task.
   b. Sub-tasks can help outline the path to success, but should not be a series of steps that tell people how to do the task.
5. The objective must be clear and the end state precise; the leader bears sole responsibility for any lack of clarity about the task.

B. **Milestones & Timelines**
1. Describe the HOW and the WHEN of the task.
2. A task with a single timeline/deadline may not need a full milestones & timelines section in the framing.
3. When the task needs periodic reviews of progress or includes specific and sequential actions the team must take, then including a detailed milestones & timelines section is strongly advised.

C. **Resources**
1. Resources encompass anything the team may need access to in order to accomplish the mission: funding, additional people, equipment, supplies, facilities, and so on.
2. Where resources are a prerequisite to mission accomplishment, the leader needs to ensure the team knows what resources are available.

3. Resources are simply enumerated within the framing by class and quantity available. Any limitation or absence of specific resources should also be defined here to preclude the team from presenting task solutions that are not feasible.

4. Task timelines are sometimes dependent upon the availability of resources.

D. Authorities

1. This section is particularly important if the task is being executed within "fuzzy" organizational lines; clarifying the authorities ensures all stakeholders understand the teams' prerogatives and limits.

2. Clear definition of authorities helps alleviate the two "Sins of Authority Misuse."

    a. Sin 1: People trying to exercise authority they do NOT have.

    b. Sin 2: People hesitating to use authority they DO have, usually because they are not confident they have it. NOTE: People who do know they have the authority, but are afraid to use it, are sending a clear message that they are wrong for the task. The leader should step in and replace them.

3. When necessary, this section should clarify succession plans, including how and when authorities can be transferred to back-ups.

IV. When tasks are dynamic, the framing needs to account for this.

A. The end state cannot always be defined at the start of the task.

1. In those cases where an end state cannot be clearly defined, conditional framing will allow the task to evolve as it progresses through a series of stages.

2. Determining what the right end state should be may even be a milestone within the task itself.

    B. The use of **branches and sequels** within a framing can be very useful in a dynamic task
       1. Branches allow a team to take an alternate direction when they hit roadblocks they cannot overcome.
       2. Sequels allow a team to "reinforce success" and accelerate their timelines when they over-achieve on a milestone.
    C. Leaders who anticipate a task will be highly dynamic should ensure they have regular progress reviews with the team so key decisions about where to go next can be made in a timely manner.
    D. Leaders should NOT over-complicate a framing by incorporating elements that support dynamic tasking when the task clearly does not require it.

Chapter 4: Building a Deep Bench

Principle #2 Know your People
&
Principle #3: Hire for Quality

I.   ***Good leaders must know their people***
    A. Within the Leading to Win model, this means building a skills profile on each person
       1. Some leaders focus on learning personal details about their people as a precursor to building a professional skills profile, and this a perfectly valid strategy if it fits the leader's personal style.
       2. However, leaders must beware of assuming that knowing their people on a personal level automatically gives them the needed insights for the professional skills profile.
    B. To know their people well, leaders must spend time with their people in the workplace
       1. If the entire team works in the same limited workspace, then this will happen naturally.

2. If subordinates work in dispersed work centers, then leaders should plan meetings and visits to those work centers as this provides the leader with more opportunities to observe their subordinates.

3. Group training and mentoring sessions are another good means for a leader to observe his team members' aptitudes.

4. Best way to assess a skill is to watch the subordinate perform a task that requires it.

II. A skills profile is built by assessing a person's strengths, gaps and weaknesses.

    A. When a person has the ability to perform a certain skill well, that is a **strength.**

    B. When a person lacks the innate skill to perform a task, but demonstrates a likely potential to be able to develop that skill, then it must initially be assessed as a **gap**. Gaps have the potential to become strengths.

        1. Often the gap can be bridged with training or targeted mentoring.

        2. Leaders can also seek **stretching** opportunities to test their team members. The stretch task should be one where a failure will not cause a significantly adverse impact to the organization.

    C. A skill that a person does not and clearly never will possess is assessed as a **weakness.**

        1. Everyone has weaknesses, so properly recognizing them allows the leader and the team to focus on gaps that have real potential to become strengths.

        2. When a skills profile indicates someone has too many weakness relative to the number of strengths, then it is incumbent upon the leader to steer that person into a more appropriate career path which may not even be in the same organization or career field.

III. Leaders who know their people well can often use that knowledge to customize their framings.
    A. If a leader knows the person to whom the task will be assigned, then that leader can draft the framing so it speaks directly to the personality of the tasked person.
        1. This approach allows the leader to add context or draft the framing text in such a way that the tasked person will feel a personal connection to the task.
        2. This personal connection often inspires a stronger commitment to accomplishing the mission on the part of the tasked person.
    B. However, if a leader has an incorrect or incomplete assessment of their subordinate's personality or skill profile, then a customized framing can cause unintended outcomes or outright mission failure.

IV. Leaders need to assemble teams with diverse capabilities.
    A. Teams whose members have a variety of skills and abilities will be well-positioned to deliver on a broader range of tasks than a team that has a lot of people with similar profiles.
    B. Leaders can sometimes fill skills gaps in the team by developing exiting team members or by doing an internal swap with another team.
    C. When leaders work in organizations where new team members are chosen by others, they can often influence the process by writing unambiguous job requirements.

V. When leaders need to add new members to the team, they must Hire for Quality
    A. Hiring for quality is a two-phase process.
        1. A quality applicant is one who has the demonstrated ability to perform the day-to-day responsibilities of the role well. An applicant who does not meet the core criteria should be set aside.

2. A quality hire is one who also brings to the team additional skills and experiences the leader is specifically seeking.

B. Every interview is an opportunity to find a prospective team member who brings unexpected skills the team lacks; leaders must take full advantage of the opportunity.

Chapter 5 The Right Choice

Principle #4: Put Your People in a Position to Succeed
&
Principle #5: Don't Put Your People in a Position to Fail

I. Choosing the right person to accomplish a task is Leading to Win's most important decision.

C. Leaders use skill set profiles to look for ideal *opportunities* to align subordinate's skills with a task's requirements.

D. This decision depends upon two distinct, but related principles.

1. "Put Your People in a Position to Succeed" describes a leader taking positive actions to bring about positive results. The leader's goal is to *intentionally align* a task's requirements with the team members' strengths to create the conditions where those strengths can be used to their fullest.

2. "Don't Put Your People in a Position to Fail" is a defense against *negative results*. The leader is aiming to *avoid* a mismatch between a task's "must have" requirements and a team member's weaknesses, so as to *prevent failure*. A person without the needed skills should be excluded from the task.

II. A great leader must orchestrate the management of task assignments when there are multiple tasks at play which can affect the outcomes of one another.

A. Principles #4 and #5 act as handrails that can channel a leader to optimal task assignment decisions in complex circumstances.

   1. Leaders must ask if assigning a task to a specific person will set the person up to fail.
      a. Unless the answer to the question is an unqualified "NO," that person *cannot* be the right choice.
      b. The goal of this step is to narrow the field of candidates to a "short list."
   2. A leader should then ask if assigning a task to a short list candidate will put that person in a position to succeed.
      a. If the answer is "NO," then that person cannot be the right choice.
      b. In most cases, the answer will lean toward the positive, but it can include comments that indicate the strength of that positive (Example: "No doubt" is stronger than "Highly likely.")
      c. The goal of this step is to use the qualified answers as a means of rank-ordering the candidates to identify the best choice.
   3. The leader may still choose not to assign the single best person to a task for various reasons, including:
      a. The need to accomplish multiple tasks simultaneously, with the realization each team member can do only one. The leader must optimize his assignments here.
      b. Recognition that the best candidate has been tasked too much lately, which can lead to burnout of that person or resentment from other team members.
      c. The desire to enable a specific team member to earn a win on the task.
   4. Putting someone without the **commitment** to win on a task—even when that someone has an otherwise ideal skill set for the task – is ultimately setting that person up to fail.

III. When a team member successfully accomplishes the mission, the leader needs to celebrate the win by recognizing the person who delivered it.

    A. Receiving honest acclaim is a big motivator for almost everyone. Recognition can boost confidence and morale almost as much as achieving the win on the task.

    B. More importantly, highlighting successful task achievement to leaders *above* is an important developmental step for the person who won on the task.

        1. The leaders above will be most able to help the person move into positions higher up in the organization.

        2. Broadcasting the credit to senior leaders demonstrates the person has gained experience and competence and is now more ready to ascend to one of those positions.

APPENDIX 1

Exhibit A: U.S. Military Ranks

Army/Air Force/Marine/ Space Force Officers	Grade	Navy/Coast Guard
General of the Army/Air Force (5-star)	*	Fleet Admiral (5 star)
General (4-star)	O-10	Admiral (4-star)
Lieutenant General (3-star)	O-9	Vice Admiral (3-star)
Major General (2-star)	O-8	Rear Admiral—Upper (2-star)
Brigadier General (1-star)	O-7	Rear Admiral—Lower (1-star)
Colonel	O-6	Captain
Lieutenant Colonel	O-5	Commander
Major	O-4	Lieutenant Commander
Captain	O-3	Lieutenant
1st Lieutenant	O-2	Lieutenant, Junior Grade
2nd Lieutenant	O-1	Ensign

** 5-star ranks are special wartime ranks only*

Air Force Enlisted Ranks

E-9 Chief Master Sergeant (CMSgt)
E-8 Senior Master Sergeant (SMSgt)
E-7 Master Sergeant (MSgt)
E-6 Technical Sergeant (TSgt)
E-5 Staff Sergeant (SSgt)
E-4 Senior Airman (SrA)
E-3 Airman First Class (A1C)
E-2 Airman (Amn)
E-1 Airman Basic (AB)

NOTE 1: Enlisted personnel in grades E-1 to E-4 are collectively called "airmen."

NOTE 2: All enlisted personnel of the sergeant ranks are formally classified as "non-commissioned officers" (NCOs).

NOTE 3: Personnel in grades E-7 to E-9 are also considered *Senior NCOs*

Exhibit B: Hierarchy of Military Units (with typical rank of the commander)

<u>Air Force:</u>

Major Command (General)
Numbered Air Force (Lieutenant General/Major General)
Wing (Brigadier General/Colonel)
Group (Colonel)

> *A group is a consolidation of squadrons with similar missions, e.g., operations group, maintenance group, mission support group, medical group, etc.*

Squadron (Lieutenant Colonel/Major)

> *A squadron is a unit composed of all the capabilities needed to execute a specific functional mission, e.g., fighter squadron, communications squadron, transportation squadron, etc.*

Flight (Captain/ Lieutenant)

<u>Army</u>

Numbered/Named Army (General)*
Corps (Lieutenant General)*
Division (Major General)
Brigade (Brigadier General/Colonel)

Regiment (Colonel)**
Battalion (Lieutenant Colonel/Major)
Company (Captain/Lieutenant)

* Civil War Union armies and corps were commanded by major generals because this was the top rank authorized in the U.S. Army at the time. Congress promoted Ulysses Grant to lieutenant general in 1864 when President Lincoln appointed him commander of all Union forces.

** In the Civil War armies, brigades were comprised of regiments, but in the modern Army, regiments are no longer subordinated to brigades; a unit commanded at the O-6 level may be a brigade or a regiment

APPENDIX 2

Exhibit A: Make the Right Choice Worksheet

Task:

S = Strength   G = Gap   W = Weakness   ------------>

CANDIDATE 1

	S	G	W
1			
2			
3			
4			
5			
6			
7			
8			
9			
10 *Dedication to the task (Critical)*			

Am I putting candidate in a Position to _Fail_ ?   Yes --> ☐   ☐ <-- No

Am I putting candidate in a Position to *Succeed* ?   Yes --> ☐   ☐ <-- No

Comment or Qualifier? ------------>

APPENDIX 2

CANDIDATE 2			CANDIDATE 3			CANDIDATE 4		
S	G	W	S	G	W	S	G	W

Yes --> ☐ ☐ <-- No Yes --> ☐ ☐ <-- No Yes --> ☐ ☐ <-- No

Yes --> ☐ ☐ <-- No Yes --> ☐ ☐ <-- No Yes --> ☐ ☐ <-- No

3

Exhibit B: Example of Completed Worksheet

<table>
<tr><td colspan="2">Task: Execute a competetive bid process to select and implement an equipment maintenance contract</td><td colspan="3" align="center">George</td></tr>
<tr><td colspan="2">S = Strength   G = Gap W = Weakness ------------></td><td>S</td><td>G</td><td>W</td></tr>
<tr><td>1</td><td>Project Management (Critical)</td><td>X</td><td></td><td></td></tr>
<tr><td>2</td><td>Technical Knowledge of Asset Management Processes</td><td>X</td><td></td><td></td></tr>
<tr><td>3</td><td>Effective Negotiator of Terms and Conditions</td><td>X</td><td></td><td></td></tr>
<tr><td>4</td><td>Life Cycle Cost Analysis</td><td>X</td><td></td><td></td></tr>
<tr><td>5</td><td></td><td></td><td></td><td></td></tr>
<tr><td>6</td><td></td><td></td><td></td><td></td></tr>
<tr><td>7</td><td></td><td></td><td></td><td></td></tr>
<tr><td>8</td><td></td><td></td><td></td><td></td></tr>
<tr><td>9</td><td></td><td></td><td></td><td></td></tr>
<tr><td>10</td><td>Dedication to the task (Critical)</td><td></td><td></td><td>X</td></tr>
<tr><td colspan="2" align="center">Am I putting candidate in a Position to <u>Fail</u> ?</td><td colspan="3">Yes --> [X] [ ] <-- No</td></tr>
<tr><td colspan="2" align="center">Am I putting candidate in a Position to <u>Succeed</u> ?</td><td colspan="3">Yes --> [ ] [ ] <-- No</td></tr>
<tr><td colspan="2" align="center">Comment or Qualifier? -----------></td><td colspan="3" align="center">N/A</td></tr>
</table>

Martha			John			Abby		
S	G	W	S	G	W	S	G	W
	X		X			X		
X				X		X		
X			X			X		
X			X				X	
X			X			X		

Martha	John	Abby
Yes --> [X] [ ] <-- No	Yes --> [ ] [X] <-- No	Yes --> [ ] [X] <-- No
Yes --> [ ] [ ] <-- No	Yes --> [X] [ ] <-- No	Yes --> [X] [ ] <-- No
N/A	If we have the right subject matter experts	Should be Fine

Exhibit C: Instructions for Using the Worksheet

Step 1: Summarize the Task

Draft a short description of the essence of the task. Use action verbs to help highlight likely skills that will be required to complete the task.

Note that in the example worksheet, the fictional leader—whom I'll call Sam – is assigning a task to acquire and onboard a maintenance contractor at a key facility. The task involves selecting the contractor, negotiating and formalizing the contract terms, and then transitioning the facility to the new maintenance model. This will be a large and lengthy task with a lot of moving pieces, and the results will matter a great deal to the organization.

Step 2: Identify the task's key skills requirements

List the skills required to do the task. Identify any skills that are critical, and list the skills in the approximate order of importance. There is room for ten skills, but unless the competition among candidates is very close, then four or five specific skills are usually sufficient. No matter how many other skills are identified, note that skill #10 must always be **Dedication to the task,** which is critical.

Sam identifies four key task requirements, one of which—project management – is rated critical. For a task of this size, a longer list of required skills would not be unreasonable, but Sam decided to focus on the few that will be most important, which is an equally valid approach.

Step 3: Assess each candidate against the task requirements

Grade each candidate against each skill. Select **STRENGTH** when the candidate has the known ability to perform that skill. Select **WEAKNESS** when the candidate is known to lack the ability to do that skill. Choose **GAP** when the candidate's ability to execute that skill is an unknown. Leaders should use judgment here and have a bias against selecting gap unless they believe the candidate will be able to bridge the gap to get the job done. If a leader has doubts about that, then the skill is better graded as a weakness. However, if the skill is of secondary importance for task completion, then leaders can be less rigid in their scoring decision and mark the skill as a gap in spite of a little doubt.

In this case, three candidates are strong project managers, but Martha is an unknown. Sam chooses to rate this skill as a GAP for Martha, indicating Sam has a high confidence Martha can do this critical skill, even though she is still unproven. Sam uses similar logic for grading John a GAP on the second skill, which is also very important. Sam gives Abby the benefit of the doubt on the least important skill, giving her a GAP even though Sam's confidence Abby can manage that skill isn't nearly as high as it was for Martha and John. Sam only assigns one WEAKNESS, and that is to George because Sam has heard George criticize the outsourcing decision that led to this task on multiple occasions, and so Sam has grave concerns about George's dedication to a project he doesn't even believe in.

Step 4: Apply Principle #5

Looking at the scores above, ask "Am I putting this candidate in a position to fail?" Generally, if any critical skills are weaknesses, or too many skills are not strengths, the answer should be "Yes."

Sam has to conclude George would be in a position to fail because of his WEAKNESS on the critical dedication skill, in spite of the fact he is clearly the overall strongest candidate on the core skills required for the task. Sam also concludes that even though Martha <u>could</u> prove to be an effective project manager, she does not earn an <u>unqualified</u> "No" on this question, so she must be a "YES." John and Abby have strong enough profiles overall to earn a No rating here and move on to the next phase.

Step 5: Apply Principle #4

For the candidates marked "No" in Step 3, ask, "Am I putting this candidate in a position to succeed? Each leader must use instinct to make this assessment, looking at the overall profile of the candidate and using their knowledge of that candidate. If the answer is "Yes," which it usually will be at this stage, then the leader may also enter a comment in the field to indicate the strength of confidence in the "Yes" assessment.

Sam does not need to assess George or Martha on this step — hence the "N/A" in the comments—because they were eliminated at the prior step. Sam determines both John and Abby will succeed, but the comments indicate that John's ability to succeed is dependent upon assigning other project members who can backstop his lack of proven technical competency. Overall, Sam clearly believes that Abby will perform well, and even sees this as an opportunity to stretch her cost analysis skills so she'll be better prepared for other tasks where this may be a critical skill.

Step 6 Make the Right Choice

Look at the comments entered in Step 5 to mentally "rack and stack" the remaining candidates. This will usually yield the single best candidate. However, the leader also has to factor in any other considerations, such as competing tasks that need to be assigned, the workload of the top candidate, or a development opportunity for another candidate. The right choice is ultimately whatever the leader determines will help maximize wins for the entire team.

Sam's own comments helped make this an easy final decision. Abby is the best candidate, but John would be viable, too. Sam must now consider any other outside factors that would weigh against choosing Abby or in favor of choosing John. In this case, there are none, and so Sam concludes that Abby is the right choice.

APPENDIX 3

Throughout the book, I referred to several of my Air Force assignments, but these references were often out of chronological order. To enable readers to see my entire Air Force career, I have attached the following two-page career history, showing my progression up the ranks and all of my assignments.

Exhibit A: Company Grade Assignments[*]

RANK		ASSIGNMENT
Cadet	1984-1988	Air Force Cadet/Student U.S. Air Force Academy Colorado Springs, Colorado
2nd Lieutenant	1988-1990	Officer-in-Charge, Vehicle Management & Officer-in-Charge, Aerial Delivery/Terminal Services 7th Mobile Aerial Port Squadron McChord AFB, Washington
1st Lieutenant	1990-1993	Port Duty Officer & Officer-in-Charge, Airlift Information Systems 619th Military Airlift Support Squadron & 619th Aerial Port Squadron Hickam Air Force Base, Hawaii
Captain	1993-1994	Chief of Transportation & **Commander**, 35th Logistics Support Flight 35th Wing Naval Air Station, Keflavik, Iceland
	1994-1997	Logistics Support Officer Headquarters 19th Air Force and Logistics Staff Officer Headquarters Air Education & Training Command Randolph Air Force Base, Texas
	1997-1998	Student Advanced Studies of Air Mobility Ft Dix, New Jersey

---

[*] *Company Grades* in the Air Force are the ranks of 2nd lieutenant, 1st lieutenant and captain, but I also included my four years as an Air Force Academy cadet on this table.

Exhibit B: Field Grade Assignments[*]

RANK	ASSIGNMENT	
Major	1998-1999	Student Air Command and Staff College Maxwell Air Force Base, Alabama
Major	1999-2001	**Commander** 375th Transportation Squadron Scott Air Force Base, Illinois
Lieutenant Colonel	2001-2004	Joint Logistics Staff Officer Headquarters U.S. European Command Patch Barracks, Germany
Lieutenant Colonel	2004-2006	**Commander** 437th Aerial Port Squadron Charleston Air Force Base, South Carolina
Lieutenant Colonel	2006-2007	Student National War College Ft McNair, District of Columbia
Colonel	2007-2009	Director for Logistics Headquarters Alaskan Command Elmendorf Air Force Base, Alaska
Colonel	2009-2010	**Commander** 455th Expeditionary Mission Support Group Bagram Airfield, Afghanistan
Colonel	2010-2012	Vice Commander 21st Expeditionary Mobility Task Force McGuire Air Force Base, New Jersey

[*] *Field Grades* in the Air Force are the ranks of major, lieutenant colonel, and colonel.

END NOTES

1   Posted 20 January 2022 at linkedin.com/pulse/top-10-best-leaders-20th-century-jan-benedict-steenkamp/

2   Ken Blanchard and Spencer Johnson, *The One Minute Manager* (New York: Harper Collins Publishing, Inc., 1981), p. 27.

3   Combined Chiefs of Staff Directive for Operation OVERLORD, 12 February 1944 para 2.

4   George S. Patton, *War as I Knew It* (Boston: Houghton-Mifflin Co., 1947), p. 357.

5   James H. Doolittle, *I Could Never be so Lucky Again* (New York: Bantam Books, 1991), p. 352.

6   Combined Chiefs of Staff Directive for Operation OVERLORD, 12 February 1944, para 2.

7   Stephen W Sears, *Chancellorsville* (New York: Houghton Mifflin Co., 1996), pp.339, 358-359, 420, 438.

8   Combined Chiefs of Staff Directive for Operation OVERLORD, 12 February 1944, para 3.

9   The *Gospel of Matthew 28:19-20* (New International Version)

10 The *Acts of the Apostles* 1:8 (NIV) *[Italics mine]*

11 The *Acts of the Apostles* 1:4-5 (NIV) *[Italics mine]*

12 The *Gospel of Luke* 24:49 (NIV)

13 The *Acts of the Apostles* 2:1-4 (NIV)

14 The *Acts of the Apostles* 2:41 (NIV)

15 The *Gospel of John*, 20:23 (NIV)

16 Philip Henry Sheridan, *The Complete Memoirs of General P. H. Sheridan* (New York: Charles L. Webster and Co., 1888), p. 126.

17 Sheridan, p. 142.

18 Sheridan, p. 190.

19 James McPherson, *Battle Cry of Freedom* (New York: Oxford university Press, 1988), p. 778.

20 Leonard Mosley, *Marshall: Hero for Our Times* (New York: Hearts Books, 1982), p. 96.

21 Forrest C. Pogue, *George C Marshall: Education of a General* (New York: The Viking Press, 1963), p. 269.

22 Mosely, p. 187.

23 Doris Kearns Goodwin, *Team of Rivals* (New York: Simon & Schuster Paperbacks, 2005), p. 485. [*Italics* mine]

24 James D. Hornfischer, *The Fleet at Flood Tide* (New York: Bantam Books, 2006), pp 399.

25 *The Gospel of Matthew* 25:14-29 (NIV)

26 *The Gospel of Mark* 4:3-8 (NIV)

27 *The Gospel of Mark* 4:20 (NIV)

28 Extracted from the website https://www.allaboutjesuschrist.org/occupations-of-the-12-disciples-faq.htm

29 The *Gospel of Mark* 6:7-12 (NIV)

30 The *Gospel of Mark* 6:13 (NIV)

31 *The Gospel of Luke* 10:1-3 (NIV)

32 *The Gospel of Luke* 10:17 (NIV)

33 *Acts of the Apostles* 1:23-26 (NIV)

34 From *BAND of BROTHERS: E Company, 506th Regiment, 101st Airborne From Normandy to Hitler's Eagle's Nest* by Stephen Ambrose. Copyright © 1992,2001 by Stephen E. Ambrose. Reprinted with permission of Simon & Schuster, Inc. All rights reserved.

35 George C. Kenney, *General Kenney Reports* (New York: Duell, Sloan & Pearce, 1949), p. 184.

36 The *Gospel of Luke*, 9:57-62 (NIV)

37 The *Gospel of Mark* 10:17-22 (NIV)

38 The *Gospel of Luke* 9:46 (NIV) and the *Gospel of Matthew* 20:20-22 (NIV)

39 The *Gospel of John* 20:25 (NIV)

40 The *Gospel of John* 20:29 (NIV) [*italics* mine]

41 The *Gospel of Matthew* 4:20 (NIV)

42 The *Gospel of Matthew* 14:28-29 (NIV)

43 The *Gospel of John*, 13:8-9 (NIV)

44 The *Gospel of Matthew* 16:13-20 (NIV) [***bold italics*** mine]

TABLE OF ILLUSTRATIONS

Chapter 1 Introducing *Leading To Win*
Here I am as a newly commissioned 2nd lieutenant on Graduation Day, June 1, 1988
Author's personal photo.

The AETC Emblem
080320-F-JZ511-644, U.S. Air Force: www.af.mil/News/Art.aspx%3Figphoto%3D2000642130

Chapter 2 What is Great Leadership?
"Jesus in Portrait"
Original artwork by Alyx Salazar [2023]

Chapter 3 The Task
General Eisenhower meets with his paratroopers in June 1944, just before their D-Day jumps
"General Dwight D. Eisenhower gives the order of the day, 'Full victory--nothing else' to paratroopers somewhere in England, just before they board their airplanes to participate in the first assault in the invasion of the continent of Europe." [June 1944], Library of Congress: www.loc.gov/item/96522674/

On July 1, 1863, Confederate forces eventually overwhelmed the Union troops defending the roads north of Gettysburg . . .
(Edited) Map by Hal Jespersen, www.cwmaps.com, "Gettysburg Battle Map Day1" [2006] Wikimedia Commons: https://commons.wikimedia.org/wiki/File:Gettysburg_Battle_Map_Day1.png

Lieutenant General Doolittle with some of his 8th Air Force fliers
[c. 1944] U.S. Air Force: www.gannett-cdn.com/presto/2021/05/03/NNWF/8e0c22c0-74bf-460d-b950-e6f4dc0ce10d-Doolittle2.jpg?width=592&format=pjpg&auto=webp&quality=70

LSTs offloading their Cargo on the D-Day Beaches . . .
"SC 308998 Normandy Invasion." [June 1944], U.S. Naval History and Heritage Command: www.history.navy.mil/content/history/nhhc/our-collections/photography/numerical-list-of-images/nara-series/sc-series/SC-300000/SC-308998.html

Map: Stonewall Jackson's "left hook" around Chancellorsville wrecks Major General Hooker's battle plan
Author's creation [2023], Road network and troop positions and movements referenced from

— "The Chancellorsville Campaign: Situation 1800, 2 May 1863" (Map), [Date Unknown] West Point Department of History: https://s3.amazonaws.com/usma-media/inline-images/academics/academic_departments/history/AmCivWar/ACW 28.jpg
— Map by Hal Jespersen, www.cwmaps.com, "Map of Chancellorsville Battle 1/3," [2006] Wikipedia: https://en.wikipedia.org/wiki/File:Chancellorsville_May1_2.png

The Ludendorff Bridge across the Rhine River at Remagen
"The Ludendorff Bridge over the Rhine between Erpel (foreground, east side) and Remagen (background, west side) after it was captured by U.S. troops" [7 March 1945], U.S. Army Signal Corps: https://commons.wikimedia.org/wiki/File:Ludendorff_Bridge_at_Remagen.jpg

Map: Generals Hodges and Patton accelerate the crossing of the Rhine River (March 1945)
Author's creation [2023], Troop dispositions provided by Keegan, John (Ed), *The Times Atlas of the Second World War* (UK: Times Books, Ltd, 1989), Map 182/2.

"Acts 1:8" (The Great Commission)
Original artwork by Alyx Salazar [2023]

Chapter 4 Building a Deep Bench

Colonel Virgil Monti
Personal photo of the subject, [ca 1995]. Used by permission.

The C-17 Globemaster III
Airman 1ˢᵗ Class Christian Silvera, photographer [undated], U.S. Air Force: https://media.defense.gov/2022/Oct/03/2003089708/-1/-1/0/221001-F-XY111-1207.JPG

Major General Philip Sheridan
"Gen. Phil. Sheridan." [No Date Recorded], Library of Congress: www.loc.gov/item/2003670641/

General of the Army George Marshall
General of the Army." [1946], Wikimedia: https://commons.wikimedia.org/wiki/File:General_George_C._Marshall,_official_military_photo,_1946.JPEG

President Abraham Lincoln confers with Major General George McClellan Shortly Before the Battle of Antietam . . .
Gardner, Alexander, photographer. "Antietam, Md. President Lincoln and Gen. George B. McClellan in the general's tent." [October 3, 1862], Library of Congress: www.loc.gov/item/2018666252/

Admirals Raymond Spruance, Marc Mitscher and Arthur Davis with their boss, Admiral Chester Nimitz
"NH 49705 Admiral Raymond A. Spruance, Vice Admiral Marc A. Mitscher, Fleet Admiral Chester W. Nimitz and Vice Admiral Willis A. Lee, Jr. (listed from left to right)" [c. 1944], U.S. Naval History and Heritage Command: www.history.navy.mil/content/history/nhhc/our-collections/photography/us-people/l/lee-willis-a-jr/nh-49705.html

General Robert E. Lee
Vannerson, Julian, photographer. "Portrait of Gen. Robert E. Lee, officer of the Confederate Army," [March 1864], Library of Congress: https://lccn.loc.gov/2018666540

Lieutenant General Richard Ewell
"Richard Stoddert Ewell, -1872, bust portrait, facing right; in uniform. CSA general." [Between 1861 and 1866], Library of Congress: www.loc.gov/item/2006681380/

Change of Command at Bagram 2010 . . .
Author's personal photo. Used with permission of all subjects.

"Matt 25:14-29" (The Parable of the Talents)
Original artwork by Alyx Salazar [2023]

Chapter 5 The Right Choice
Then a major, I assumed command of the 375th Transportation Squadron at Scott Air Force Base in 1999 . . .
Author's personal photo.

Emblem of Colonel Robert Sink's 506th Parachute Infantry Regiment
"506th Infantry Regiment." The Institute of Heraldry, U.S. Army: https://en.wikipedia.org/wiki/506th_Infantry_Regiment_(United_States)

I was deployed to Baghdad on short notice in 2006 while a lieutenant colonel . . .
Author's personal photo.

As a Cadet First Class in Fall 1987, I commanded Cadet Squadron 2 . . .
Author's personal photo.

General MacArthur personally decorating Lieutenant General George Kenney for the Air Force's actions during the Battle of the Bismarck Sea
[February 8, 1944] Australia @ War Collection: https://www.ozat-war.com/ozatwar/kenney.htm. (Used by permission of site creator Peter Dunn)

Now both retired from the Air Force, Colonel Virgil Monti and I are reunited at Randolph Air Force Base in 2023 in front of the Logistics Directorate building where we worked together from 1995-1997
[March 31, 2023] Author's personal photo.

"Matt 4:19" (Jesus calls Peter)
Original artwork by Alyx Salazar [2023]

"The Dome of St Peter's Basilica"
Original artwork by Alyx Salazar [2023]

ABOUT THE AUTHOR

Chris Pike was born in 1966 and grew up in Connecticut. In 1984 he fulfilled a childhood dream and entered the U.S. Air Force Academy. He graduated four years later with majors in Military History and International Affairs and a commission as a second lieutenant in the U.S. Air Force. Unable to attend pilot training due to vison deficiencies, Lieutenant Pike became an air transportation officer so he could lead Airmen executing the military airlift mission. He spent the next 24 years on active duty, working across a spectrum of missions and programs, primarily associated with transportation and logistics. He retired in 2012 at the rank of colonel. During his career Colonel Pike had 13 assignments to nine U.S. states—including both Alaska and Hawaii—and three foreign countries. He also deployed to Riyadh, Saudi Arabia, in 1991 for the Gulf War and to Baghdad, Iraq, in 2006 in support of Operation IRAQI FREEDOM. Colonel Pike commanded two Air Force squadrons and from 2009-2010 he served as commander of the 455th Expeditionary Mission Support Group at Bagram Airfield, Afghanistan. Several months after retiring from the Air Force, Chris and his family moved to Houston to take a job managing logistics within the corporate sector. This myriad of experiences led him to develop the leadership model he describes in *Leading to Win.*

In addition to his Bachelor of Science degree from the Air Force Academy, Chris holds four masters degrees, and is a graduate of the Air Command and Staff College and the National War College. He has always been an avid reader and traveler, and he has maintained his passion for history his entire life, continuously researching topics throughout the discipline. He hopes *Leading to Win* will be the first of several publications.

Chris and his wife Libby just celebrated their 25th wedding anniversary. They are proud parents of a daughter and a son, both of whom are full-time college students. The Pikes live in The Woodlands, Texas.

www.ingramcontent.com/pod-product-compliance
Lightning Source LLC
Chambersburg PA
CBHW070836160726
48004CB00001B/404